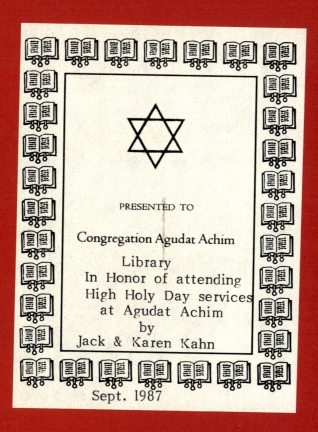

# The Jokes of Oppression

## The Humor of Soviet Jews

# The Jokes of Oppression

## The Humor of Soviet Jews

David A. Harris
Izrail Rabinovich

Jason Aronson Inc.
*Northvale, New Jersey*
*London*

10 9 8 7 6 5 4 3 2 1

**Library of Congress Cataloging-in-Publication Data**

Harris, David A.
  The jokes of oppression : the humor of Soviet Jews / David A.
Harris, Izrail Rabinovich.
    p.      cm.
  Includes bibliographical references.
  ISBN 0-87668-993-4
  1. Jewish wit and humor. 2. Jews—Soviet Union—Anecdotes,
facetiae, satire, etc. 3. Soviet Union—History, comic, satirical,
etc. 4. Soviet Union—Ethnic relations—Anecdotes, facetiae,
satire, etc. I. Rabinovich, Izrail. II. Title.
PN6231.J5H37   1988
891.78'0244'08—dc19                                                87-30805
                                                                    CIP

Manufactured in the United States of America.

To Jou Jou, Danny, Mishy, and Josh,
and my mother, Nelly Harris,
and in loving memory of Ida, Lova, and Yuli Chender

To my parents, Samuel and Dora Rabinovich

# Contents

# Introduction

Few Westerners realize how vital a role political humor plays as a commentary on society and an emotional outlet for people behind the Iron Curtain. Deprived of opportunities for self-expression at the ballot box, in the press, assembly, or cultural forms, political humor becomes a treasured, if largely private, means of conveying anger, frustration, or criticism in an often hostile environment.

Two million Soviet Jews, finding themselves unable to live as Jews or to leave the country in substantial numbers, turned early on to humor as a means of coping with the extraordinary pressures and tensions in their daily lives. Essentially, they drew on the anecdotes, vignettes, and stories of Jews who have lived in Russia since time immemorial. Some of these will be immediately recognizable in the West; others incorporate the poignant black humor that is so much a feature of daily life in every Communist country.

Soviet Jews are in fact another example of a remarkable historical phenomenon: "The People of the Book," confronted with centuries of relentless persecution, keep turning to humor to seek solace, diversion, and affirmation, thus becoming, in a sense, "The People of the Joke." As Leo Rosten wrote in the introduction to his classic book, *The Joys of Yiddish,* "In nothing is Jewish psychology so vividly revealed as in Jewish jokes."[1]

---

[1]Leo Rosten, *The Joys of Yiddish,* New York: McGraw-Hill, 1968, p. xxiv.

The jokes compiled in this collection are the product of a collaboration that began more than a decade ago in Rome. At the time, as the result of a chance meeting in the office of the Hebrew Immigrant Aid Society, the international agency that assists Soviet and other Jewish migrants, we learned that each of us—an America-bound refugee from Moscow, who had been a professor of South Asian studies, and a native New Yorker, who was working as a HIAS migration counselor—had a common interest in recording the rich and, in the West, little-known humor of Soviet Jews.

Within three months, we were separated by 4,000 miles and never again saw one another; but we exchanged hundreds of letters containing literally thousands of jokes in Russian, which we duly translated into English and filed. The jokes came entirely from our contact with Soviet Jews in the USSR, from those in transit in Austria and Italy, and from many others who resettled in Israel, the United States, Canada, and England. They were heard in meetings, at weddings, on the beach, in cafes and shops, in taxis, and in private homes. Soviet Jews are wonderful storytellers, especially, according to tradition, those from the Ukrainian port city of Odessa, home to a large Jewish community and a once-flourishing Yiddish culture. Good jokes are savored, indeed treasured, and rapidly passed along via the "Jewish telegraph."

As word of our interest spread, many people sought us out to share their stories, some in person and others in written form. Our files bulge with tattered pieces of paper inscribed with jokes offered to us by Soviet Jews. Some of the material, for reasons of language or context, simply proved untranslatable. Puns, rhymes, and many historical references and cultural allusions seldom survived the effort to render them into English.

The stories included in this collection, likely to be understood even by those with only a minimal knowledge of Soviet life, were chosen to illustrate how Soviet Jews have used humor as an important vehicle in the face of second-class citizenship and discrimination. Humor becomes, together with faith, pride, and a national identity moored in 4,000 years of history, a primary weapon in the admittedly limited, but still potent arsenal of Soviet Jews, a prized mechanism for coping with life's myriad difficulties.

Indeed, one might well say that the Soviet ideological machinery has no more fearless and resilient foe than the Jewish joke. It is an adversary that fears neither the jails nor the prison camps. It seemingly travels at the speed of light, easily escapes detection by the KGB or militia, and has even less difficulty eluding the Soviet defense apparatus than Mathias Rust, the 19-year-old West German pilot who flew unscathed in 1987 from Finland to Red Square. It penetrates every social pore in the country, from the local sobering stations to the Kremlin itself. The Jews may not be free in the Soviet totalitarian world, but the Jewish joke is.

Can we vouch for the pedigree of each and every story as an original, authentic product? It would be impossible. Stories move too easily across national and ethnic boundaries. Those familiar with Israeli and East European humor, for example, will find many striking similarities to the material in this collection. Furthermore, we claim to be neither humor genealogists nor cultural anthropologists; our goal was not a scientific study of Jewish humor from the Soviet Union. Rather, our cue, perhaps, was taken from the late E. B. White, who once warned: "Humor can be dissected, as a frog can, but the thing dies in the process and the innards are discouraging to any but the pure scientific mind."[2] Consequently, we have been content to include all material with one common denominator—that it was recounted to us by Soviet Jews who considered many of the jokes as their own. In addition, we hope, in the process, to provide a comprehensible and entertaining insider's look at some of the most notable features that have characterized seventy years of Soviet and Jewish life in the USSR.

Such a collection of humor is not only an encyclopedia of Jewish life; inevitably, it is also an encyclopedia of Soviet life in general. It might even be possible to write a history of the seventy years of the Soviet state through the recounting of these jokes alone. In Soviet

---

[2]Quoted in *Time* 87:9 (March 4, 1966), p. 46.

society, with its innumerable prohibitions, jokes—particularly Jewish jokes—become one of the rare accurate reflections of actual conditions. And so the Western reader should be prepared. Not all jokes are meant to be funny per se. Many have a bittersweet, poignant, or self-deprecating side. Entertainment is only part of their purpose.

Most other genres of societal commentaries have enjoyed shorter life spans. Russian historical events were once reflected in folk songs and legends; and in the first third of the twentieth century, two- and four-line folk verse, usually topical and humorous, became a popular art form; but the only genre to survive intact all these years as a mirror of life's realities has been the joke, Jewish as often as not.

Of course, Jewish humor quickly outgrew ethnic limitations. It was embraced by Russians, Ukrainians, and Georgians, among others, as the ultimate expression of discontent with the status quo. Moreover, it provided the impetus for such other pseudonational forms of Soviet anecdotes as "Armenian Radio," or "Radio Yerevan." In fact, this form of political humor, which is characterized by questions and answers, is not at all Armenian but rather Jewish (and Russian) in origin, having made its first appearance in Moscow.

The book is organized loosely into four sections. In Part I, which comprises more than half the book, the focus is on Jewish political humor. The reader will note several recurring themes in the material that address key issues in Soviet Jewish life: pervasive anti-Semitism that Jews encounter on the streets, in offices and factories, at schools and in the media; the desire to emigrate; pride in Israel's lightning victory against Soviet-backed Arab forces in the 1967 Six-Day War and a subsequent belief in the Jewish state's invincibility; alternating feelings of superiority and inferiority in response to discrimination and hostility; and the proverbial wisdom of the rabbi, no matter what the circumstances.

Other themes, primarily contained in Parts I and II (general political humor), derive more generally from some of the well-known features of Soviet life: impatience with a labyrinthine and hostile bureaucracy; discontent with quality, quantity, and service in consumer life; fear of the KGB; memories of decades of Stalinist terror; the ubiquitousness of the Communist party; turbulent relations with China and the U.S.; frustration at the absence of incentive in a suffocatingly centralized economic system; and a healthy disrespect for the quality of the country's leadership.

Part III consists of what might be termed universal and eternal Jewish jokes recounted to us by Soviet Jews. Likely as they are to have largely originated on Russian or adjoining East European soil, many of these jokes have made their way west and will strike a familiar sound among readers. And finally, Part IV offers a representative sampling of true stories involving Soviet Jews in the USSR, in transit, or in their new countries of resettlement. They are drawn from the authors' own experiences.

Throughout all the post-1917 humor, the central hero of the Jewish joke—poor Rabinovich, or for variety's sake, say, Shapiro or Khaimovich—manages to face life with endless reserves of common sense and optimism, and conjures up, perhaps, the richest oral image in the USSR. How ironic that in a country where the Communist party embarked on a vicious anti-Semitic campaign in the decades after World War II, seeking to arouse the worst prejudices of Russians and other nationality groups against the Jewish minority, a slight, shy, insignificant, everyday Jew—a Rabinovich—could capture the imagination of Soviet Jews and non-Jews alike and could become the irrepressible foil of the world's most powerful repressive society.

Those who have spent time in the USSR, in the company of local citizens, know that when Russians or Jews or Armenians meet together, it never takes long before they start exchanging the most recent Jewish and other political jokes. Party leaders and dissidents, professors and taxi drivers, prison wardens and government ministers have all been known to relish the latest anecdote. Moreover, Soviet leaders from Lenin to Gorbachev have reportedly all been afficionados!

There was one issue, however, that troubled us during the book's preparation, namely, how to handle those jokes that might be considered offensive to a particular ethnic or religious group. In the end, we engaged in some self-censorship. Our goal has been to avoid the gratuitous denigration of any people. We have, nevertheless, included some examples of what might be regarded as mild ethnic stereotyping, both of Jews and others, especially where they attempt to make an instructive point. Quite frankly, such humor is so much a part of Soviet life—where more than 100 nationalities can be counted—that we would be remiss were we not to offer at least a few illustrations. However, we wish to make absolutely clear that we intended no offense by their inclusion.

Notwithstanding Soviet claims of a genuine brotherhood among the many nationalities in the country, the reality is, not surprisingly, far more complex, as it is in any pluralistic society. Generalizations abound, and antagonisms linger; but as Alan Dershowitz, professor of law at Harvard University, wrote in a 1987 syndicated column, "Jokes, by their very nature, are necessarily provocative, upsetting and stereotypical—at least to some. Humor . . . is in the eye, ear and psyche of the beholder."[3]

This book could never have been compiled without the help of literally hundreds of Soviet Jews living in a half-dozen countries. They are simply too many in number to even attempt to recall their names here—the university student from Odessa en route to Australia; the taxi driver from Lvov, currently living in St. Louis; the machinist from Kharkov, now working at an Israeli aircraft factory; the English-language teacher in Moscow; the pensioner from Leningrad, finally reunited with his children in New York. In a very real sense, this is *their* book. Their contributions are reflected on every page, borne out of bittersweet experiences in a land that has proved inhospitable to those Jews in its midst who sought to live their lives as Jews and as free human beings.

---

[3] Alan Dershowitz, "Joke Law Isn't Funny," *This World, San Francisco Chronicle* (March 30, 1987), p. 16.

Moreover, we are grateful for the steadfast and unremitting support that we have received from our respective families over many years. Our infinitely patient wives—Giulietta Boukhobza and Irina Petrovna Rabinovich—served as our most reliable sounding boards. Invariably, we would try out every new story on them, and they fulfilled this unsought role with consummate grace, critical sense, and yes, humor.

Finally, we wish to express deep appreciation to Arthur Kurzweil, Jason Aronson's editor-in-chief, whose faith in this project and professional talent have been crucial to its completion, and to his exceptional editorial production team, especially Muriel Jorgensen; to Leonard Fein, founding editor of *Moment*, and Marc Silver, editor of the B'nai B'rith International *Jewish Monthly*, for having given us confidence and encouragement by publishing excerpts from our collection even before we could envision a book; to Dr. Yoram Dinstein, Nehemiah Levanon, and Yehoshua Pratt—three stalwarts of Israel's decades-long efforts in behalf of Soviet Jewry—who shared with us several jokes included in our book; and to Kevin Klose for an anecdote that he heard from Soviet Jews while serving as the *Washington Post's* outstanding Moscow correspondent in the late 1970s.

The secret source of Humor itself is not joy but sorrow. There is no humor in heaven.

—Mark Twain

# WARNING

WARNING: The authors of this book have determined that reading this book may be harmful to your health . . . in the Soviet Union!

GUARANTEE

GUARANTEE: Possession of this book in the USSR will result in up to eight years' imprisonment . . . or your money back.

# PART I

## Jewish Political Humor

Shortly after Abram[1] left Kiev for a business trip to Eastern Europe, his friend back home received a telegram from Poland: GREETINGS FROM FREE WARSAW, ABRAM. A few days later a second telegram, this one from Czechoslovakia, arrived: GREETINGS FROM FREE PRAGUE, ABRAM. Several more days passed before a third telegram, from Hungary, came: GREETINGS FROM FREE BUDAPEST, ABRAM. A long period of silence followed before the friend in Kiev received a telegram from Israel: GREETINGS FROM JERUSALEM, FREE ABRAM.

Gorbachev received a present of very expensive material for a suit from a foreign leader. He went to all the best tailors in Moscow to have the suit made, but at each shop, he met with the same response: "There simply isn't enough material to make a two-piece suit."

---

[1]Typically Jewish first names, including Abram, Khaim, Moishe, and Sarah, and surnames such as Abramovich, Khaimovich, Rabinovich, and Shapiro identify Jewish protagonists. Ivan and Petya are among the most common first names and Ivanov and Petrov the most common surnames used in the jokes to identify those of the numerically most populous Russian nationality.

Finally, having exhausted all the tailors in Moscow, Gorbachev went to Odessa. Fortunately, he ran into Khaimovich, an old tailor, who agreed to make the suit. In a few days' time, Gorbachev returned to Khaimovich's shop to find that not only had a two piece suit been prepared, but also a vest and even a cap were made from the same material.

"Comrade Khaimovich, how is it possible that you managed to make the suit, a vest, and a cap from the material I gave you when all the tailors in Moscow insisted that there wasn't even enough material to make a two-piece suit?"

"Comrade Gorbachev, in Moscow, you're a very big man; but frankly, here in Odessa, you just aren't that big!"

A Russian, a Ukrainian, and a Jew were summoned to appear at Communist party headquarters on the same day.

"Comrades," said the party leader, "you are surely aware that you may soon be called upon to sacrifice your very lives for your beloved motherland and for the father of our country, Leonid Ilich Brezhnev. Should this be so, do you have any last wish?"

The Russian and Ukrainian remained silent.

"I do," said the Jews. "Just a small one. Couldn't I be left as an orphan instead?"

A meeting of personnel directors of the local offices and factories was called by the local party committee to discuss the difference between a Zionist and a Jew. The party spokesman began to inveigh against Zionism, Zionist infiltration in all walks of Soviet life, and Zionist aims internationally.

"But, comrade, could you please explain how we personnel officers can distinguish between such a demonic Zionist as you have described and a simple, everyday Jew?"

"It's really very simple, comrades. Surely, you have many Jews working in your offices and factories, and there is no problem with them. They are all normal members of our Soviet society. But a Zionist can readily be identified as any Jew who comes to your personnel office looking for a job."

Three prison inmates were locked in the same cell; they soon began talking.

"What are you here for?" asked one inmate of another.

"They put me in for beating up some old Jew named Khaimovich," snarled one man.

"And why are you here?" asked the second of the first.

"For having defended some old Jew named Khaimovich in a fight," he replied.

"And what were you arrested for?" the third inmate was asked.

"For being Khaimovich," he sighed.

Khaimovich was at Moscow's airport going through customs on his way to Israel.

"You," barked the customs official at Khaimovich, "why are you taking this picture of our beloved leader with you if you're emigrating?"

"Oh that. That's in case I get homesick for the Soviet Union," he explained. "All I have to do is look at the picture, and I'll be cured of the homesickness."

In a class at the Soviet War College, the following exchange was overheard.

"Professor, I have a question. How can we, 260 million people, ever rebuff an attack by almost one billion Chinese?"

"That should be easy. Why, just look at how a mere three million Jews in Israel have handled 100 million Arabs."

"Yes, you're absolutely right—but where are we going to find three million Jews to fight the Chinese for us?"

There was a knock at the door of Shapiro's apartment at 3 A.M. He buried his head under the pillow, but the knocking persisted. Reluctantly, he put on his slippers and robe and went to the front door.

"Who is it?" he asked.

"The postman," came the unexpected reply.

Shapiro opened the door and was promptly set upon by five hulking KGB agents.

"Tell us, Shapiro, what is the greatest country in the world?" they demanded.

"Our homeland, of course," said Shapiro.

"And what is the best political system yet invented?" the interrogators continued.

"Communism," replied Shapiro without hesitation.

"And in what country do workers enjoy real freedom?" they queried.

"The Soviet Union," sighed Shapiro.

"Then tell us, Shapiro, why have you applied to emigrate to Israel?" they shouted.

"Because at least *there*," Shapiro yawned, "the postman doesn't wake you up at 3 A.M."

The Kharkov District Party Committee wanted to deter Jews from gathering at the synagogue. On Rosh Hashanah, the Jewish New Year, a notice was posted on the synagogue's main door: CLOSED DUE TO HOLIDAY.

In the USSR, everyone aged 16 and older must have an internal passport. In the year 2000, the Kremlin predicts, a new Soviet passport will be issued to reflect the fact that the ultimate goal of Communism has been achieved: All the 100-plus nationalities in the USSR will have been joyously blended into one group—the Soviet people. Thus, the authorities will finally be able to eliminate all references to nationality. The new passport will look like this:

```
Surname:_____

First Name:_____

Father's Name:_____

Date of Birth:_____

Nationality during period of socialist transition:
Jewish or non-Jewish (circle one)
```

Solomon Isaakovich Abramovich was called to the factory office.

"Abramovich, we must fire you," said the manager.

"But why? I'm not a Jew, I'm a Russian. Here, look at my passport," protested Abramovich.

"That's just the point," replied the manager, somewhat annoyed. "If we already employ a man named Solomon Isaakovich Abramovich, at least he should have the courtesy to be a Jew!"

"What's your name, little boy?" asked the policeman.

"Abram," he replied.

"Imagine that—so young and already a Jew!" the officer wondered aloud.

*Question:* Why are there no Jewish cosmonauts?

*Answer:*    The Soviet authorities are afraid they would never return.

Khaimovich applied to emigrate from the USSR. He was called to OVIR[2] and notified that his application had been refused.

"But why?" protested Khaimovich.

"Because you are in possession of state secrets from your place of work," explained the OVIR official.

"State secrets? You must be kidding. In my field, the Americans are at least twenty years ahead of us!" he exclaimed.

"That's *precisely* the secret," came the curt reply.

---

[2]Visa Office.

"Soviet intellectual development is much more advanced than that of the Israelis," said the director of Odessa OVIR to his wife. "For example, in Israel, the debate about 'Who is a Jew' has been going on for decades; but in our office, we can decide the question in no more than five minutes."

After submitting an application to emigrate, Rabinovich was duly summoned to OVIR.

The harangue began. "Rabinovich, how could you possibly want to go to a country like Israel? Do you realize that the sun is so strong in the summer that you won't be able to stand it? And in the winter it does nothing but rain. The climate is just awful."

The OVIR official continued in the same manner for several more minutes while Rabinovich did nothing but sway from side to side, muttering to himself, "Yes, no, yes, no, . . . "

"Excuse me, Rabinovich, but can you please explain to me why you're acting in this strange manner?" the official interrupted.

"Sure," came the answer. "On the basis of what you were saying, I was simply trying to decide whether or not it would be worthwhile to take my umbrella with me."

And yet another time, Rabinovich was called to OVIR to discuss his application to emigrate to Israel.

"Isn't everything good for you here, Rabinovich? Don't you have all that you need?" asked the OVIR official.

"Well," began Rabinovich, "the fact of the matter is that I have two reasons for wanting to emigrate. The first is because of my neighbor. Every night he comes home stone-drunk and starts cursing the Jews. He is always saying that as soon as the Communists are overthrown, he and his Russian friends will go out and hang all the Jews."

"But, Rabinovich, you know that we Communists will never be overthrown," said the official smugly.

"And that," said Rabinovich, "is exactly my second reason."

Khaim was finally granted permission to leave Russia. He emigrated to Israel but returned to Odessa after a few months. Then he emigrated again to Israel, but again was back in Odessa before too long. And then he emigrated to Israel yet a third time; but predictably, he returned to Odessa within a few weeks.

"Khaim, why did you leave the USSR in the first place?" his friend Abram asked.

"Because life here was just terrible," he sighed.

"But then why did you leave Israel?" Abram retorted.

"Because I didn't speak a word of Hebrew, and the weather was just too humid for me," Khaim whined.

"Then why do you insist on going back and forth between two countries in which you're unable to live?" the friend asked, bewildered.

"Because of the wonderful stopover in Vienna!" Khaim laughed.

Abramovich was summoned to OVIR.

"Why, Abramovich? Why do you want to leave us, to leave the land that nurtured you?" the official inquired.

Abramovich remained silent.

"Don't you have a job?" the official asked, as he began enumerating with his fingers.

"I do," Abramovich whispered.

"And don't you have a place to live for a very cheap rent?" the official continued.

"I do," mumbled Abramovich.

"And free medical care?" the official noted.

"That too," sighed Abramovich.

"And schooling for your children?" the official confronted Abramovich.

"Uh-huh," the poor Jew agreed.

"Then why could you possibly want to leave, you dirty Jew?" bellowed the official.

"You've just reminded me, comrade. Thank you," smiled Abramovich.

A Jewish wife in the Soviet Union is not a luxury but a means of international transport.

You know, of course, that there are two groups of Jews in the Soviet Union: first, there are the brave—those who leave the country, and then, there are the *very* brave—those who don't!

Did you hear that the Russians have been claiming that the Jews are the lucky ones? They complain, "After all, the Jews have a country of their own, somewhere they can go; but to what country can we Russians emigrate?"

Some years ago, Brezhnev and Kosygin met to discuss the Jewish question in the Soviet Union.

"Kosygin, how many Jews do we have here?" asked the General Secretary.

"About two million, I think," replied the premier.

"I have an idea. Why don't we open the borders to let out the troublemakers among them? That will serve two purposes: We'll be rid of an internal problem, and we'll also win some public relations points in the West. What do you think?" asked Brezhnev eagerly.

"Fine, fine idea," responded Kosygin.

"And how many Jews do you think would actually leave?" queried Brezhnev, raising his eyebrows.

"Probably no less than five million!" said Kosygin earnestly.

Once again, Khaimovich was called to the OVIR office.

"Khaimovich, I want to know why you've decided to leave the country," asked the OVIR official.

"No, no, you've got it all wrong. I don't want to leave; my *wife* does," he hastened to explain.

"So divorce and let her emigrate by herself," the official advised.

"Yes, but—it's not quite that simple. It's not only my wife who wants to leave, but also her mother," Khaimovich continued.

"So, what's the problem?" asked the official, annoyance written all over his face. "Let those bloody Zionists go. We don't need them here, do we Khaimovich?"

"Yes, well—but then there's also my wife's brother's family, and then there are my wife's in-laws and their other children," the Jew stammered.

"So, they'll go—and you and I will remain to build Communism," the official said emphatically.

"But there's still a problem," Khaimovich interjected.

"What?" demanded the official.

"They can't leave without me. I'm the only Jew among them!" came the reply.

"Khaim, what would you do if the borders were opened tomorrow?" asked Abram.

"I'd jump into the nearest tree," Khaim promptly replied.

"But why?" asked Abram, wrinkling his brow.

"So as not to be run over by the stampede, of course," Khaim answered.

While visiting the USSR, a delegation of American industrialists asked to see a factory. The Soviet hosts selected a suitable one and arranged with the factory manager for the committee to visit early the following week. The factory manager set about getting everything in perfect order. Suddenly, to his horror, he realized that he didn't have a *single Jewish employee* in the plant. "How will I respond if the Americans ask to meet a Jew?" he worried. "After all, they are always going on about the Jews in Russia and how they are being discriminated against," he groaned.

An idea flashed into mind. Hurriedly, the manager called a handful of employees into his office. He explained the plan to them. "You will be issued new passports for the next couple of days listing you as Jews. This way, even though none of you employees looks particularly Jewish, you can all show your passports to any of the Americans as proof that you are, in fact, Jews."

The delegation came and inspected the factory. The plan worked perfectly. A week later, the manager summoned the "Jewish" employees to his office to give them back their old passports, but none of them could be found.

He called his assistant.

"Where are they?" he demanded.

"Uh, uh . . .," hesitated the assistant.

"Out with it!" the manager shouted.

The assistant mumbled, "They've all emigrated to Israel."

Khaimovich had a parrot. One day while he was at work, the neighbors heard the parrot saying: "We are fed up with this socialist paradise. We want to go to Israel." The neighbors promptly called the KGB. Several agents arrived and waited for Khaimovich to return home from work. When he finally came home, the agents warned him that if the parrot continued to make such anti-Soviet remarks, there would be a lot of trouble for Khaimovich and the parrot.

Khaimovich, being a wise man, decided to put the parrot in the refrigerator overnight. The next morning, the KGB agents returned and demanded to see the parrot. When Khaimovich opened the refrigerator door, the parrot, without a moment's hesitation, began to shout: "Down with Zionism. Up with Marxism-Leninism. Down with Zionism. Up with Marxism-Leninism." The KGB agents were satisfied and left.

Khaimovich turned to his parrot and said: "I'm very glad to see that one night in the refrigerator made you realize how things would have been for us in Siberia."

Returning to New York from a trip to the Soviet Union, Goldberg, a member of the U.S. Communist Party, was summoned to the local headquarters.

"Comrade Goldberg, did you have the chance to meet any real, unshakable Marxists during your three-month official tour of the Soviet Union?" a party boss inquired.

"Only one," came the terse reply.

"And who was that?" the official queried.

"Kogan, another tourist from New York," said Goldberg.

*Question:* Do you know Khaim, the fellow who lives across the street from the prison?

*Answer:* Yes, but now he lives across the street from his house.

"My Khaim is such a storyteller," boasted Sarah. "Why, a few years ago, he was sentenced to three years for telling just one anecdote, and last night, he told an anecdote that was worth at least eight years!" she beamed proudly.

Store director Rozenblit was arrested and charged with embezzlement of state funds. After being found guilty of the charge, he was permitted to send a telegram to his wife in the Crimea. Afraid to further incur the wrath of the authorities, he cautiously composed the following text: SOVIET JUSTICE HAS ONCE AGAIN TRIUMPHED. The next day, he received a reply from his wife: FILE AN APPEAL IMMEDIATELY.

A competition of hammer throwers was held. All the best Soviet athletes participated, but the competition was won by Khaimovich, a frail Jewish pensioner.

"Khaimovich, how could you possibly have thrown the hammer far enough to win the competition?" asked a journalist.

"If you give me a sickle," replied Khaimovich, "I'll throw *it* even farther."

Abram telephoned the KGB.

"Hello. Is this the KGB headquarters? I was just wondering whether by any chance a parrot has come to your office," Abram inquired.

"No," came the reply.

"Well, if he should come, I just want to let you know in advance that I don't share his political views," Abram explained.

*Question:* What is the longest street in Odessa?

*Answer:* Bebelya Street, without a doubt.

*Question:* Why?

*Answer:* Because Abramovich went down it five years ago to KGB headquarters, and he still hasn't returned.

"Shapiro, we know you have a brother abroad," said the KGB official.

"I do not," Shapiro protested vehemently.

"Don't lie to us, Shapiro. We even have these letters from him addressed to you and postmarked Jerusalem," the official sneered.

"Ah, you don't understand," explained Shapiro. "It's not my brother who is abroad; it is I!"

To show the world the true egalitarian spirit of the Soviet Union, an orchestra comprised of representatives of various nationalities was organized. At a Moscow press conference, each member was individually introduced to the foreign journalists by the conductor, Sergei Ivanov.

"This is Fyodorov the Russian," he began. "And this is Murzhenko the Ukrainian, Saroyan the Armenian, and Chikvili the Georgian. And here is Rabinovich the violinist."

In response to Khrushchev's appeal to Soviet youth to participate in the development of Siberia's virgin lands, a Moscow party chief summoned a meeting of Komsomol[3] leaders.

"Comrades," he began. "I want you to set the example for our young people. Go and live in Siberia. Experience for yourselves the true joy of living. Discover the privileged reality of a genuine Communist life-style. Who will make the commitment?" he asked eagerly.

To the party chief's surprise, no one volunteered. Again he implored, but to no avail. In desperation, he decided to speak to the Komsomol leaders individually; but each had a ready excuse: health, family, studies. Finally, he approached Abram.

---

[3]The Communist youth and young adult organization.

"Abram, I know you well," the chief said, placing his hand on Abram's shoulder. "I know that you're healthy, that your family is fine, and that you've finished all your studies. Why don't you volunteer?"

Without hesitation, Abram spoke up. "You yourself said that to go to Siberia was a true privilege and a real joy. Just imagine for a minute what would happen if I would volunteer to go. Everyone here would *again* complain that it's the Jews who get all the best opportunities!"

An advertisement appeared in a Soviet newspaper: "Prepared to exchange one Jewish nationality for up to two pending prison sentences."

*Question:* What does friendship among Soviet nationalities mean?

*Answer:*   It means that the Armenians take the Russians by the hand; the Russians take the Ukrainians by the hand; the Ukrainians take the Uzbeks by the hand; and they all go and beat up the Jews.

As soon as Abram arrived in Moscow, he cabled his wife Bertha at home in Berdichev: DON'T TELL THE KGB ABOUT THE BOX HIDDEN IN THE GARDEN. To Abram's delight, the message was intercepted, and the KGB rushed to his home equipped with bulldozers and shovels. While the agents were digging up the garden, Bertha frantically ran to the nearest phone to call her husband in Moscow.

"Abram, are you crazy?" she cried, almost hysterical. "The KGB is ripping apart our land."

"Don't worry, my dear," Abram calmed her over the phone. "I only wanted to make the spring planting easier for you."

Ivan desperately needed to urinate but was unable to find a public toilet. Looking around and seeing no one, he hurriedly went up to the wall of the nearest building.

Poor Ivan. He hadn't noticed that this wasn't just *any* building, it was the Odessa headquarters of the Communist party. A militiaman spotted him and came running.

"Citizen, you must pay a fifty-kopeck fine for violating the public order," demanded the militiaman.

Ivan, feeling lucky to have gotten off so lightly, obediently reached into his pocket and pulled out a one-ruble note. The policeman didn't have the necessary change.

"Listen," apologized the militiaman, "I don't have the fifty kopecks change to give you now; but I'll be on guard again tomorrow night, so you just come over, and I'll give you another pee on the house."

Shortly after Abram returned home after three years' confinement in a prison camp in the notorious Magadan region, his neighbor besieged him with questions about life in the camp. Abram, however, was less than anxious to talk about the experience.

"Okay, okay," Abram finally said. "I'll tell you what it was really like. We used to wake up before the crack of dawn. *Do you know why?* Because it's good for the health.

"Then, no matter what the weather was like, we would take a cold shower outdoors. *Do you know why?* Because it improves the circulation.

"Then we had breakfast. Granted, it was a simple breakfast, but *do you know why?* Because a rich diet is bad for the heart.

"After breakfast, we walked eight miles to the forest, worked the entire day without interruption, regardless of the weather, and then we walked the eight miles back to the camp. *Do you know why?* Because the long walks and the outdoor work are good exercise, the landscape is beautiful, and it prepares you for a restful sleep.

"In the evenings, there were lectures on sociopolitical topics. *Do you know why?* Because these lectures serve to broaden your cultural and political horizons."

"But Abram, that all sounds very peculiar to me," remarked the neighbor. "I was talking to another fellow about a month ago—a guy named Khaim Shapiro—and he told me some very different things about his camp experience. By any chance, did you ever meet him while you were in camp?"

"Yeah, I met him," Abram sighed, "and just as I was leaving the camp, I saw the guards bringing him back for a second term. *Do you know why?*"

A bus was traveling along one of the main streets of Kiev. The conductor was calling out the stops: "Boulevard Shevchenko."

"Pre-revolutionary Bibimovsky Boulevard," shouted one of the passengers, contradicting the conductor.

At the next stop, the conductor announced, "Lenin Street."

"Pre-revolutionary Fundukleevskaya Street," commented the same passenger.

At the next stop, the conductor hollered, "Sverdlov Street."

"Pre-revolutionary Proreznaya," exclaimed the passenger.

"Citizen Jew, pre-revolutionary Jew-bastard," bellowed the conductor, "kindly shut up and stop disturbing my work."

Rabinovich walked up to a stranger in the street.

"I have a favor to ask you," he said. "Please give me a punch in the mouth."

"But why?" asked the startled stranger.

"Let me explain. A few minutes ago, a complete stranger came up to me and asked: 'Are you planning to emigrate to Israel, dirty Jew?' I said, 'Yes, I am.' He called me a traitor to the Soviet Union, punched me in the mouth, and walked away.

"Then another passer-by came up and asked me if I was planning to emigrate to Israel. This time, of course, I said, 'No, I'm not.' He told me there was no place in the USSR for dirty Jews, hit me in the mouth, and walked away.

"Then a third passer-by approached and asked if I was a member of the party. I said, 'Yes.' He told me there was no place in the party for Jews, hit me in the mouth, and walked away.

"Then a fourth person came up and asked me if I was a member of the party. This time, of course, I said, 'No.' He accused me of being disloyal, hit me in the mouth and walked away.

"So do me a favor and hit me already, but just don't ask any questions. I'm sick and tired of the questions."

Khaimovich went for a job interview. The personnel officer asked him to sit with his side to the desk. He then proceeded to glance back and forth, back and forth, between Khaimovich's face and his application

form. After a few minutes, the officer declared: "Comrade Khaimovich, I can see from your profile that you're just not the right man for
us."

A man came to ask the rabbi a question.

"Rabbi, what is Communism?" he inquired.

"My friend," replied the rabbi, "it's like a taxi ride."

"I don't understand, Rabbi," said the man apologetically.

"Ah," sighed the rabbi. "The longer we go on, the more we pay."

Another inquiry was made of the rabbi.

"What is a brake?" the rabbi was asked.

"A brake," responded the rabbi, "is the *moving force* of the Soviet
socialist system."

The conductors of the Odessa and Philadelphia philharmonic orches-
tras met.

"We have two Jews in our orchestra," remarked the Odessa
conductor. "How many do you have?"

"We don't count them," replied the Philadelphian.

Imagine that you are at the Moscow circus in the year 2050. The
ringmaster steps into the center ring. A hush falls over the arena.

"Ladies and gentlemen," booms the voice of the ringmaster. "For the first, and probably only time in your lives, the Moscow circus proudly presents for your viewing pleasure a real live Jew!"

Two drunken fellows were walking down an Odessa street.

"Vasya, why don't we try and smash the atom?" asked the first.

"Nah," Vasya replied, "it's too much trouble. Let's smash the window of Khaimovich's shop instead."

It turned out that the two men who were assigned to Room #37 in the resort hotel in Sochi were both employees of the same bank.

"How difficult my work is!" complained one. "I have so much to do. I don't even have a moment's rest from morning 'til evening."

"What are you talking about?" interrupted the other. "Take it from me, I don't work more than a couple of hours a day. Whenever a piece of paper is sent my way, I don't even bother reading it. I just write 'For Rabinovich' on the top and send it along."

"And I," sighed the first, "am Rabinovich."

It happened aboard a domestic flight in the Soviet Union.

"You two over there, shut up," barked the stewardess at passengers Khaimovich and Shapiro. "You damned Jews are making a racket; you're disturbing the other passengers."

One hour later, the plane landed in Odessa.

"Do we now have your permission to speak?" Khaimovich and
Shapiro meekly asked the stewardess.

"Yes," she replied.

"Good. We wanted to tell you that Rabinovich fell out of the
plane an hour ago," they said, as they exited from the aircraft.

In court.

"Will the defendant state his name for the court," intoned the
judge.

"Solomon Abramovich Shapiro," was the reply.

"Where was the defendant born?" asked the judge.

"Berdichev," the defendant said.

"What is the defendant's profession?" the judge continued.

"Tailor," replied Shapiro.

"And what is the defendant's nationality?" the judge droned on.

"And what do you think I am, *Mongolian?*" retorted Shapiro.

The Soviet space program provides this scenario.

"Calling mission control, calling mission control. This is Cosmonaut Khaimovich. Confirm my present position."

"Khaimovich, you jerk! How many times have we told you? Here
in your homeland you may be a Khaimovich, but in space you are the
'Soviet eagle.'"

Khaim was walking down the street when someone called him a
Jew-bastard.

Under his breath, Khaim muttered, "Ay! If only there were meat in the shops, it would be just like in the times of the last tsar, Nicholas II. I would have still been a Jew-bastard, but at least then there was meat!"

Stalin summoned a Russian, a Ukrainian, and a Jew to his office in the Kremlin.

"You, Ivanov, I want you to go out on the balcony and throw yourself to the ground eight stories below to demonstrate your willingness to sacrifice your life for me," ordered Stalin.

Ivanov hesitated.

"You, Komarenko, I want *you* to jump," Stalin commanded.

Komarenko froze.

"You, Khaimovich, I want *you* to jump."

Khaimovich rushed to the balcony and was just about to throw himself over when Stalin stopped him. "Khaimovich, you've now demonstrated your loyalty to me. Tell me, what led you to act so decisively?" asked the perplexed Stalin.

"Frankly, I prefer a terrible end to endless terror," explained Khaimovich.

After a lecture by a senior official at party headquarters, a discussion took place.

"I would like everyone's personal comments on the speech just given by our party comrade from Moscow," said the local party chief to the rank and file. "Ivanov, what do you think?"

"A brilliant speech," responded Ivanov.

"Petrov?" the chief queried yet another man.

"Outstanding," came the loyal reply.

"Koramenko?" the official continued.

"I can't even begin to find the right words to express my admiration for the speaker," gushed Koramenko.

"Kogan, why are you so quiet?" inquired the party leader. "Don't you have an opinion on the speech?"

"I do, but unfortunately I don't agree with it," answered the Jew.

Grinberg was one of a very small number of Soviet emigrés who joined Rakah, the Israeli Communist party. His friends back in the USSR couldn't help but laugh at the irony. In Odessa Grinberg had been considered "a dirty Jew," but in Tel Aviv he was suddenly regarded by the Kremlin as an "eminent Israeli Communist."

*Question:* Why is there a monument in Israel to the first Soviet cosmonaut, Yuri Gagarin?

*Answer:* Because as his space capsule was about to take off, he declared: "Let's get going." More than 275,000 Jews have taken his advice so far.

The Grinbergs emigrated from Odessa to Tel Aviv, where they opened a small restaurant. Mr. Grinberg had been a cook in an Odessa eatery. One day in the kitchen, she noticed that every so often he would grab a piece of meat, wrap it in newspaper, and quickly stuff it into his pocket.

"David!" shouted his wife. "What do you think you're doing? Remember this is *your* restaurant."

"Oh, Sarah, I had completely forgotten," he replied.

Nixon, Brezhnev, and Golda Meir were sitting together on a plane when God announced to them that a worldwide flood would begin in three days to punish mankind for its sinfulness. He advised the three leaders to return to their respective countries immediately.

Nixon rushed to Washington and made a nationwide television broadcast in which he announced that the world would end in three days. For the next three days, he ordered, America's capitalists would not have to contend with any government controls; they were permitted to make all the money they wanted.

Brezhnev, on the other hand, told the Soviet people that inasmuch as there were only three days left, they could assume that the final stage of Communism had been reached, and they were given permission to drink unlimited vodka.

Golda Meir optimistically went before the Knesset to advise the parliamentarians that there were only three days left for government leaders to come up with a feasible plan to make it possible for the people of Israel to continue living underwater!

*Question:* Why isn't there a Communist government in Israel?

*Answer:* And why should a small country have such a big joy?

A secret meeting took place between Soviet leader Brezhnev and Israeli Prime Minister Begin. Brezhnev magnanimously promised to seek Arab recognition of Israel on the condition that Begin persuade President Carter to return Alaska to Russia.

A planeload of Soviet Jewish immigrants arrived at Tel Aviv's Lod Airport. As they disembarked, each joyously held up both hands with the "V" sign.

"Victory! Victory!" shouted the frenzied Israeli crowd assembled to meet the new arrivals.

"What are you people talking about?" said a spokesman for the arriving group. "We want our villas and Volvos."

A Jew went to the local rabbi to seek his sage counsel.

"Rabbi," he began, "my son is going to be drafted into the Red Army tomorrow. Help us so that he won't have to go."

"Tell your son that he should stay up all night reading from the Talmud," the sage advised.

The next day the man returned to the rabbi and complained bitterly, "Rabbi, my son did just as you said. He stayed up all night reading from the Talmud, but this morning they came anyway and took him into the army."

"But did he get a hernia during the night?" asked the rabbi.

"No," replied the irate father.

"Well you see," explained the rabbi, "my prescription doesn't work unless you also get a hernia during the night."

Two Jews were in the Yeliseevsky food shop in Odessa. How elegant and well stocked it had been before the revolution!

"Ah, Khaim, do you remember that corner over there? That's where they sold black caviar," said Abram, pointing to a stall where potatoes were now displayed.

"Yes, Abram. And don't you remember that corner over there? That's where they sold such delicious red caviar," said Khaim, pointing to an egg stand.

"Ay, ay, ay. Just tell me, Khaim, did the caviar really get in anyone's way?" Abram asked sadly.

Brezhnev went for a visit to the so-called Jewish Autonomous District of Birobidzhan. At a collective farm named "The Dawn of Communism," he inquired about the year's harvest.

"About average," explained Khaimovich, the farm's spokesman.

"What does *average* mean, Comrade Khaimovich?" the Soviet leader asked.

"It means worse than last year's and better than next year's."

Dora met Sara carrying a big bundle on an Odessa street.

"I see that you've already done your shopping," observed Dora.

"On the contrary," moaned Sara, "I'm just about to do it. These bottles are for the sunflower oil, the cans are for jam and sour cream, the pot for salted cucumbers, the newspaper to wrap the cabbage, and I'll stuff the potatoes and beets in my pockets."

A consumer update from the USSR.

"Izrail Abramovich, is there any meat?" a customer asked the shop clerk in Odessa Supermarket No. 1.

"There's no meat," he replied.

"And where *can* I locate some?" persisted the customer.

"I was told confidentially," whispered Abramovich, "that there's a place not too far from here. It's about twelve hours away."

"What's the place called?" pleaded the customer.

"New York," the clerk sighed.

For the literary-minded, this anecdote is revealing.

"Yesterday, Khaimovich and his wife from Apartment 7 were arrested," said Petrov to his wife. "Just imagine, they were hiding anti-Soviet literature. And they seemed like such honest Soviet citizens!"

"Those Jews are all the same," said the wife. "Exactly what kind of literature was found?"

"A prerevolutionary cookbook. We're not supposed to know about all the wonderful foods they had before 1917!" the husband explained.

Abram and his wife were going through customs before boarding a plane for Vienna.

"Do you have any gold with you?" the customs official asked Abram.

"Yes, I do. I have sixty kilos," Abram responded sincerely.

"It's against Soviet law to take gold out of the country. You will have to leave it here," the official instructed.

"Sarah, my golden, I'm afraid they won't let you out," Abram explained to his precious wife.

No sooner did the newspaper kiosk open every morning than Shapiro rushed to buy the paper, scanned the first page, and threw the paper away in the nearest litter basket. The newspaper vendor couldn't quite figure out the reason for this strange behavior and decided to ask Shapiro about it.

"Citizen, what is it that interests you in the paper?" asked the vendor.

"Obituaries," replied Shapiro.

"But obituaries are listed on the back page, not the first," said the vendor.

"Believe me," said Shapiro, "the obituary that I'm waiting for will be printed on the first page."

Khaimovich was asked whether he thought that the most pressing problems dividing the Soviet Union and China could be resolved by the beginning of the next century.

"I believe," began Khaimovich with an air of authority, "that all the most pressing problems dividing the Soviet Union and China will be solved by the beginning of the next century—with the exception of only one."

"Which?" he was asked.

"Who will rule the Eurasian land mass," Khaimovich declared.

They say that Brezhnev is a great collector of Jewish anecdotes; he's already collected two prison camps filled with them.

Another hint about the state of human rights in the USSR.

"Citizen Shapiro," the OVIR official ceremoniously announced to the applicant for emigration, "you have received permission—to stay in the Soviet Union."

Rabinovich was called to OVIR to discuss his emigration application.

"Tell me, Rabinovich, to what country do you want to emigrate?" asked the OVIR official.

"To Israel," came the prompt reply.

"All right," said the official, calculating that pensioner Rabinovich was only a drain on the Soviet economy.

Two days passed. Rabinovich returned to OVIR to seek out the official with whom he had spoken earlier. "Excuse me, comrade, but I've changed my mind. I can't go to Israel. You see, it's a country in need of young people and, in any case, the climate is much too warm for me."

"So where have you decided to go?" the OVIR official asked.

"To America," Rabinovich stated firmly.

"All right, Rabinovich. For us, there's no problem," the official assured him.

Another two days passed. Rabinovich again returned to OVIR to speak with the same official. "Comrade, all those things that one reads in the newspaper about crime, inflation, and urban decay in the United States have convinced me that I wouldn't be very well off there. I've decided to go to France."

"Listen, Rabinovich, I hope that this time you've really made up your mind because I'm beginning to lose my patience," the official said sharply.

"This time I'm 100 percent sure," Rabinovich promised.

But Rabinovich wasn't so sure, because within 48 hours he was back in the official's office. "Comrade," began Rabinovich without the slightest hint of embarrassment, "I have decided that France is not for me. All those beautiful women and that good wine would be too much of a temptation for an old man like me. . . . "

"I've had it," interrupted the official. "Look, take this globe into the next room, study it carefully, and then return here within fifteen minutes, and tell me what country you've chosen. This is your *last chance*."

A few minutes passed before Rabinovich returned to the official's office. "Ah, Rabinovich, you've finally decided, have you?" the official beamed.

"No, comrade," sighed the weary Jew, "I was only wondering whether you have another globe. The first one you gave me didn't seem to have anything particularly interesting to offer."

In a primary school.

"Who can tell us all about our beloved homeland, the Soviet Union, and the United States?" asked the teacher. "Abie, you tell us something."

"In the USSR, everything is good—and in America, everything is bad," dutifully replied Abie.

"Excellent, Abie," smiled the teacher. "Are there any questions, class?"

"I've got a question," said Abie. "Why is it that if everything here is so good, it's so bad? And if everything there is so bad, why is it so good?"

An office director placed an ad for a bookkeeper. Four persons responded and were all called in for interviews. He ushered the first candidate into his office.

"Tell me, how much is two times two?" the director asked.

"Four," replied the first candidate.

"Thank you, but you are free to go," he said as he thought to himself, "Such a precise person might not be willing to pad the figures." He called in the second candidate.

"Tell me, please, how much is two times two?" he again asked.

"Three," the second candidate replied.

"Sorry, I can't offer you the job," he said as he thought to himself, "A person with sights so low would never be able to fill the ambitious five-year plans set by the state." He called in the third applicant and asked the same question.

"Five," came the answer.

"Good-bye," he said as he thought to himself, "Such a person might show a propensity to take some of the extra for himself." He called in the fourth person, Rabinovich.

"Tell me, please, how much is two times two?" the director asked yet again.

Rabinovich thought for a moment, looked over the man sitting opposite him, and said, "Actually, I'm very flexible on the question. Just tell me how much you want it to be."

"You're hired," the director replied.

Two friends were sitting on a park bench.

"Khaim, why do you read *Pravda?*" asked the first.

"And how else would I learn what a happy life we lead?" retorted Khaim.

A group of Jews was seeing off their emigrating friends at Moscow's airport when the police official approached. "Mr. and Mrs. Shapiro, you are leaving for Vienna, so please be kind enough to proceed to the plane. The rest of you dirty Jews, get away from the damned gate."

Khaim and Moishe boarded a bus together but were separated by the large crowd. Suddenly Khaim saw the bus conductor approaching to check the validity of each passenger's ticket. Wanting to warn Moishe who, like himself, hadn't bothered to buy a ticket, Khaim shouted out: "Moishe, have you bought a ticket?"

"How could I?" replied Moishe. "I still haven't received my exit visa."

In a retaurant in Odessa, this conversation was overheard.

"How many Jews are there in Odessa?" asked the foreign visitor.

"500,000," replied Khaim.

"And who makes up the rest of the population?" inquired the visitor further.

"Jewesses," replied Khaim.

In the Moscow airport, this encounter took place.

"What do you have in that suitcase over there?" asked the customs inspector.

"Feed," replied Tsilberman.

"What did you say?" asked the inspector.

"I said, 'feed,'" Tsilberman repeated.

"Feed for whom?" pressed the inspector.

"Feed for Western chickens, geese, and ducks," Tsilberman explained.

"Open the suitcase," ordered the customs man.

Tsilberman did as he was told. The suitcase was bulging with diamonds, gold, and silver.

"So, this you call feed, huh?" sneered the customs inspector.

"Yes, feed. Of course, I don't know if Western chickens, geese, and ducks will eat it—you see, this is my first trip abroad—but I thought I'd bring it along to let them at least taste the stuff," Tsilberman replied.

The Soviet authorities ended restrictions on Jewish emigration from Odessa and sent a boat to the port to transport those who wished to go to Israel. Hour after hour, day after day, hundreds and thousands of Jews boarded the ship; yet still there seemed to be room for more.

"Tell me, comrade," commented a dockside observer to one of the ship's crew, "that boat's quite an amazing example of Soviet technology to be able to hold so many people. Surely it must be made of some kind of new rubber material, huh?"

"Oh no," replied the crew member, "it's really much simpler than that. You see, the boat has no bottom."

Poor Khaim. His next door neighbor was a KGB agent. Every morning the two of them would leave their apartments at exactly the same hour and Khaim would greet him with "Good evening."

This went on for months and months, until finally one morning, the agent asked Khaim, "Why is it that you always say 'good evening' to me despite the fact that we see each other at eight o'clock in the morning?"

"Because when I see your uniform, things immediately darken for me," replied Khaim.

Khaimovich and Abramovich, specialists in humor, met.

"Khaimovich, do you know the joke about the . . ." asked Abramovich.

"Oh sure, that's an old one," laughed Khaimovich.

"And the one about the . . ." asked Abramovich.

"Yes, of course," chuckled Khaimovich.

"And what about the one where Brezhnev is sitting in his bedroom, takes a gun out of his dresser, and shoots himself?" Abramovich asked.

"Wow, I've never heard that one!" said Khaimovich eagerly.

"Neither have I, but doesn't it make a great beginning?" roared Abramovich.

Khaimovich was called to district party headquarters.

"Khaimovich, we need you to manage a new international brothel that the party is planning for Moscow. The brothel is absolutely necessary for our program to get as much information as possible from and about foreign visitors and to photograph them in potentially compromising situations. To reflect the importance of this job, we are prepared to pay you a salary of 20,000 rubles per year, and you will, of course, be surrounded by beautiful women. What do you say?" asked the party official.

"Absolutely no," Khaimovich said.

"30,000 rubles per year?" offered the official.

"The answer is still no." Khaimovich remained firm.

"But why?" asked the official. "The average worker doesn't make more than 2,000 rubles a year."

"That's not the point," insisted Khaimovich. "I can foresee exactly what's going to happen. In six months' time, one of the girls is going to be called away from the brothel for advanced ideological training. In seven months, another is going to go on maternity leave. In eight months, a third is going to be called to help with the harvest on a collective farm. Before you know it, there will be no one left in the brothel but me, and you'll send me a directive, something to the effect of : 'Khaimovich, duty is duty. You must help the party out in its time of need. Get into bed yourself and fill the monthly plan for the brothel.' That's why I don't want the job."

Khaim and Abram were brothers. Khaim lived in Israel, Abram in the Soviet Union. Because they were having problems with their correspondence, Khaim wrote the following letter to Abram:

Dear Abram,

    To find out whether my letters are being censored, I am putting a hair in this envelope.

Your brother,
Khaim

A few weeks later, Khaim received a letter from Abram:

Dear Khaim,

    Rest assured that there's no censorship. I've just received your last letter with the hair in it.

Your brother,
Abram

Khaim immediately responded:

Dear Abram,

Indeed the letters are censored. I never actually put any hair in my last letter to you.

Your brother,
Khaim

Khaim and Izya met on the street.

"Khaim, did you hear that the Office for the Protection of State Property searched Abram's apartment recently?" Izya asked anxiously.

"But I just saw him yesterday," Khaim replied in a shocked tone.

"And they found gold, about eighty kilos, but shhhhh! Not a word about this to anyone," cautioned Izya.

"But I just saw him," Khaim tried to explain.

"He was arrested and tried. Shhhh!" admonished Izya.

"But yesterday . . ." Khaim tried again.

"And then he was shot," whispered Izya.

"But wait—look. There goes Abram now," Khaim said, totally confused.

"Shhh! He doesn't know about it yet!" replied Izya.

Because of the great concern in the USSR over the question of population protection in the event of a nuclear attack, Khaimovich was required to attend a course in civil defense. Then he had to take an oral examination.

"Comrade Khaimovich, what should we do in case of a nuclear attack?" asked the examiner.

"First of all, everyone should lie down," answered Khaimovich.

"But why?" asked the examiner.

"Because standing up will be out of the question," replied Khaimovich.

A young Jew was sitting on a very crowded bus. A drunk man got on the bus, stood over the young Jew, and eyed his seat. The young Jew didn't move.

"I lost my leg in the battle of Stalingrad in 1943," said the drunk.

The young man, unwilling to give up his prized seat, ignored him.

The drunk repeated himself. "I lost my leg in the battle of Stalingrad in 1943."

Still the young Jew continued to ignore him. The man persisted until the young Jew looked up and said, "What do you want from me? I haven't seen your leg anywhere."

One day all the Jewish pupils were called to the school office. The backs of their hands were stamped with the seal that quality control experts in Soviet factories reserve for the best goods.

When one of the non-Jewish pupils saw the seal, he was envious. He asked his teacher how he could get it.

"Oh, Ivan, how silly of you," explained the teacher. "You should know that the seal is always reserved for goods destined for export."

Khaim, an illiterate, was employed as a janitor in the Moscow Central Synagogue until a decree was issued by the Kremlin stating that all employed persons must be literate. The rabbi was, therefore, compelled to fire Khaim.

Seeing no other prospect for work in the USSR, Khaim applied to emigrate to the United States. Because he was uneducated, the Soviet authorities were only too happy to let him go.

In the United States, Khaim had a bit of luck, becoming a millionaire within a few years. As a result, he became a familiar and respected figure in the community.

One day, he entered a very exclusive shop and bought several thousand dollars worth of goods.

"Are you paying by check, sir?" asked the salesman with great deference.

"No, I'll pay in cash," smiled Khaim.

"But you know, sir," replied the clerk, "it would be much better if you paid by check in the future."

"That may be true for others, but not for me, young man. You see, I'm illiterate," explained Khaim.

"A man of your standing, illiterate? It's just not possible. Just imagine what you might have become had you been able to read and write!" said the clerk in awe.

"What are you carrying on like that for?" asked Khaim. "Had I been literate, I'd still be working as a janitor in the Moscow synagogue."

*Question:* What is a Soviet optimist?

*Answer:* Someone without all the facts.

The Soviet aviation industry spent millions of rubles to develop a new plane, but the test flights proved disastrous because of a problem with the wings. In midflight, they would simply break right off. Unable to find a solution to this nagging problem, and unwilling to scrap the entire project, the aviation authorities appealed to the general public for ideas. Khaimovich, convinced that he could solve the problem despite his lack of technical training, persuaded the authorities to let him have a go at it.

"All I need is a drill," explained Khaimovich.

"Just a drill? Nothing else?" asked the incredulous supervising engineer.

"No, that's all I need," replied Khaimovich.

Khaimovich proceeded to drill straight lines of holes from front to rear on both wings, and then he announced that the plane was airworthy. With great skepticism, the authorities gave the okay to the test pilot to try the plane. Miracle of miracles! The plane took off, the wings held, the pilot went through his entire routine, and the plane landed safely.

"A genius! A hero of Soviet labor! Brilliant! But how did you manage it, Khaimovich? What principle of aerodynamics did you use? Explain everything," insisted the stunned observers.

"It was actually all very simple. I used the theory of Soviet toilet paper. Wherever there are holes, the toilet paper never tears off. I assumed that the same principle would apply to the plane's wings!" said Khaimovich with a smile.

Years ago, when the attention of the Soviet people was focused on the fate of the missing Nobil expedition to the North Pole, Khaim went to the telegraph office to send a cable.

There was a long line, but Khaim went right up to the front, wrote out a telegram: KIEV. TO RABINOVICH. IMMEDIATELY SEND FIVE BOXES OF SALT. KHAIM. He then tried to give it to the clerk.

The clerk pointed out to Khaim that he would have to wait in line since only telegrams connected with the Nobil expedition were being accepted out of turn.

Khaim went away and returned to the clerk two minutes later with the following text: KIEV. TO RABINOVICH. SEARCH FOR NOBIL. IF YOU DON'T FIND HIM, IMMEDIATELY SEND FIVE BOXES OF SALT. KHAIM.

Barenboim was called to the police station.

"Your neighbor Abramovich, in the communal apartment, claims that you were a witness to the fact that in the kitchen Petrov called him a Jew-bastard and threw his soup on the floor. Comrade Barenboim, I want to warn you that you are only to discuss those things that you personally witnessed, not those things that others later told you about. Otherwise, you may be charged with giving false testimony. Now, let's begin. Comrade Barenboim, when were you born?" asked the policeman.

"I don't know," replied Barenboim.

"How can you possibly not know?" asked the officer, utterly dismayed.

"Because I didn't personally witness the event," replied Barenboim honestly.

*Question:* Why was Khaim sentenced to thirteen years' imprisonment?

*Answer:* For calling a government minister a jerk. Three of the thirteen years were for insulting a government official and the other ten were for disclosing a state secret.

At a Soviet factory, two men talked.

"Khaim, do you consider the Soviet Union a friend or a brother?" a work colleague asked.

"A brother, of course," replied the other.

"But why?" asked the first.

"Because with friends at least I can choose them," came the reply.

In a dentist's office, the following exchange took place.

"How much does it cost to get a tooth pulled in the Soviet Union?" inquired the American tourist.

"Three thousand rubles," replied Dr. Khaimovich.

"Three thousand rubles! Why so much?" asked the startled American.

"Because it isn't such an easy operation in a country where you always have to keep your mouth shut," explained the Soviet dentist.

*Question:* What is pleasure for a Russian?

*Answer:* To go with a friend to the subway, pass a sign that reads, "Spitting Prohibited. Fine: Three Rubles," and have his friend say, "Go ahead and spit, Ivan. It's on me."

Once they arrived in New York from Odessa, Sarah began to teach her son proper manners. One day they found themselves on a crowded bus.

"Yasha, you must learn to be a gentleman," said Sarah to her son. "Stand up and give your seat to that fat cow standing over there. By the way she looks, one would think that she just got off the plane from Berdichev."

Yasha stood up and managed to address a few words in English to the woman. "Sit you down, please."

"The fat cow from Berdichev thanks you," responded the woman in Russian.

Two Soviet Jewish immigrants met in New York.

"Are you set up yet?" asked one.

"No, I'm still working," replied the other.

After the Soviet-Chinese war, in the city of Hua Go-Fen (formerly Odessa) on Den Tso Street (formerly Lenin Prospect), two Chinese stood.

"Khaim, don't you agree that it was better when the Bolsheviks were here?" asked the first.

"Absolutely," Khaim replied. "At least then we didn't have to squint all the time."

Two brothers, Khaim and Moishe, emigrated from the USSR to the United States, but after a short while, Moishe became homesick for Odessa and decided to go back. However, before Moishe left, the two of them decided that Moishe would use a code to write his letters from Odessa: if things were going well, he would use blue ink; but if things were going badly, he'd use red ink.

A few weeks after Moishe's return to the USSR, Khaim received a card postmarked Odessa. The text, written in blue ink, read:

Dear Khaim,

Everything is wonderful, and I am so happy here. You can't imagine how nice people are to me. No one shows the slightest concern that I had earlier decided to leave this beloved homeland of mine. What a fool I was to ever think about leaving in the first place.

And the standard of living has risen unimaginably. The stores are stocked with just about everything; but there's only one thing I haven't found. Yesterday I went looking for red ink, but you can't find any for love or money.

Your brother,
Moishe

As Abram and Sarah passed the headquarters of the KGB in Leningrad on the tram, he sighed.

"Abram," whispered Sarah, "how many times have I told you not to carry on political discussions in public?"

The good fairy came to old Khaimovich in his sleep.

"Ask for anything and it shall be yours," said the fairy. "Your wish is my command."

"I'd like to live out my last years in the finest old age home in the country," sighed Khaimovich longingly.

His wish was granted, and suddenly, Khamovich found himself in the Kremlin in the company of Brezhnev, Kosygin, Gromyko, Suslov, and the other Politburo golden-agers.

Sarah and Tsilya met on the street.

"My son Abram is just like our beloved Karl Marx," exclaimed Sarah. "If he's not reading, he's writing, and if he's not writing, he's reading."

"My son Khaim is just like our beloved Lenin," responded Tsilya. "If he's not in internal exile, he's in prison; and if he's not in prison, he's in internal exile."

Khaim sat down at a restaurant table, ordered a brandy and asked the waiter to bring him a copy of the day's *Pravda*. The waiter brought him the brandy but no paper.

"And where's the paper?" asked Khaim.

"I'm sorry," the waiter apologized, "but there is no more *Pravda*. The government fell yesterday."

A few minutes passed, and Khaim again called the waiter, ordered another brandy, and asked him to bring a copy of the day's *Pravda*.

"I've told you already that there's no more *Pravda*. The government fell yesterday," the waiter replied, rather annoyed.

A few more minutes passed. Khaim again called the waiter, ordered another brandy, and asked for a copy of *Pravda*.

"Listen, how many times must I tell you? There is no more *Pravda*. The government fell yesterday. Can't you understand that? There is no more Soviet power," the waiter said, his voice rising in anger.

"Of course I understand it," remarked Khaim, "but I just can't hear it often enough."

Rosenfeld emigrated to Israel in 1970.

"How old are you?" he was asked by an Israeli immigration official.

"Twenty-two," was the man's reply.

"What? You must be at least seventy," said the official.

"Maybe so," replied Rosenfeld, "but can you really call the last fifty years living?"

Abramovich and Rosenberg were, respectively, Soviet and American Communists. When they died, they appeared before God. God decided to send Abramovich to heaven and Rosenberg to hell.

"But why should I be sent to hell?" protested Rosenberg. "After all, we're both Communists and deserve the same treatment. Are we both guilty or innocent?"

"Of course you're both guilty," declared God. "But Abramovich spent his whole life in hell. He, at least, deserves a view of heaven. However you, Comrade Rosenberg, haven't yet spent a day of your life there."

Khaimovich wasn't at all happy at the idea of living next to such a boorish and uneducated neighbor. One day he saw him in the lobby.

"You fool, I'll bet you don't even know who wrote *Hamlet*, do you?" he challenged.

Unbeknownst to Khaimovich, his neighbor worked for the KGB. Khaimovich was quickly arrested and taken to KGB headquarters. Nothing more was known about Khaimovich for several days until his neighbor was overheard speaking to another KGB man.

"I'm 100 percent certain that Khaimovich wrote *Hamlet*. Give me a few more days, and I'll make him confess to it," the secret agent promised.

Khaim was called to KGB headquarters and accused of having defiled the party newspaper *Pravda* by using it as toilet paper.

"No, it's not true. I categorically deny the charge," protested Khaim.

"It's not enough that you protest your innocence. We need proof," demanded the KGB official.

"You want proof? Well," said Khaim, "the fact of the matter is that I've had constipation since the Bolshevik Revolution."

Brezhnev was reported to have a recurring nightmare in the late 1960s. He saw Chinese soldiers in Czech-made tanks eating matzah and taking in the sights of Red Square.

The pilot of the Aeroflot plane stepped out of the flight cabin and into the passenger section.

"Are there any Jews on board this plane?" he shouted.

Silence.

"I said, 'Are there any Jews here,'" he repeated.

After a few minutes, a very timid voice responded, "Uh, yes I-I-I am a Jew."

"Good. To which Western country are you hijacking us?" asked the pilot.

A delegation of foreign visitors paid a visit to a Soviet school. The schoolchildren had, of course, been prepared well in advance for the visit and were only too eager to respond to the visitors' questions.

"Are pupils in the Soviet Union happy?" asked one foreigner.

"Soviet pupils are the happiest in the world," responded the class in unison.

"And are Soviet pupils well fed?" asked another visitor.

"Soviet pupils are the best-fed pupils in the world," the children dutifully answered.

"And do Soviet pupils suffer from any form of racial, religious, or ethnic discrimination?" the class was asked.

"Soviet pupils suffer from absolutely no racial, religious, or ethnic discrimination. We are all members of one big, happy Soviet family," came the choral reply.

So ended the meeting between the delegation and the class. As the visitors were filing out of the classroom, they noticed one pupil quietly crying in the back of the room.

"What's your name, young fellow?" the boy was asked.

"Abie," the child sobbed.

"And why are you crying?" they asked.

"Because I so much want to go to that wonderful country called the Soviet Union," wailed Abie.

On the occasion of Brezhnev's seventieth birthday in 1976, he received the following telegram from Khaimovich: DEAR LEONID ILICH, MAY I SAY THAT AT 70 YOU LOOK FAR BETTER THAN OUR COUNTRY DOES AT 60.

Khaim was standing on Red Square watching a very elaborate funeral procession pass by.

"Tell me, who is the funeral for?" he solemnly asked a mourner.

"For a member of the Politburo," replied the mourner.

"What a procession! I wonder how much it costs," said Khaim.

"I'd say about 1,000 rubles," came the estimate.

"One thousand rubles!" murmured Khaim. "For that kind of money I'd agree to bury the entire government."

Brezhnev and Kosygin were chatting.

"You know, Kosygin, I've heard that Jewish jokes have become very popular in our country. That's incredible! How is it possible in a country where members of all nationalities are brothers and where we will soon reach the final stage of Communism?" wondered Brezhnev.

"Brezhnev, that's the funniest Jewish joke I've heard yet!" laughed Kosygin.

Two Jews arrived at work.

"Khaim, do you have any good jokes today?" asked the first.

"No. And you, Izya?" asked the other.

"Me neither," replied the first.

"Damned, we have some dull government these days, don't we?" they both exclaimed.

An American arrived in Moscow late one evening, registered at his hotel, and then decided to go for a walk. Anxious to practice the little Russian he knew, he looked everywhere for people to talk to; but the streets of the center were completely deserted. Finally, after walking for half an hour, he came across Khaimovich.

"Excuse me, sir, but why are the streets so empty?" asked the American.

"Did you ever hear of a fellow named Solzhenitsyn?" asked Khaimovich.

"Yes, but what does that have to do with my question?" the American persisted.

"And do you know what Solzhenitsyn did for a living?" inquired the Jew.

"Yes, he was a writer, but . . ." said the American.

"And do you know what kind of books he wrote?" Khaimovich interrupted.

"Political, antigovernment, anti-Stalin books. But I really don't see how all this matters. Where are the people?" demanded the American.

"And do you know what happened to Solzhenitsyn?" the Jew continued.

"Yes, he was kidnapped and forced to emigrate to the West. Now I've been answering all your questions. Please answer *my one question*: Where are all the people?" insisted the American.

"They're all sitting at home trying to write antigovernment books," explained Khaimovich.

Ivan walked into a shop.

"You don't have any meat, do you?" he asked Khaim the clerk.

"No, here we don't have any *fish*. Next door, at the butcher's, *they* don't have any meat," replied Khaim.

A meeting of the Politburo was in session.

"Comrades," said Brezhnev to the members of the Politburo, "it's time we really do something dramatic in space. I'm sick and tired of watching the Americans upstage us. I have, therefore, ordered the preparation of a manned mission to the sun."

"But Leonid Ilich," cried out one Politburo member, "won't the capsule burn up as it approaches the sun?"

"There's absolutely no danger of that," replied the Soviet leader. "Khaimovich, a distinguished scientist, says that we can avoid the problem by sending up the capsule at night."

*Question:* What is the difference between an optimist and a pessimist in the Soviet Union?

*Answer:* An optimist believes that things have gotten as bad as they're going to get, whereas a pessimist believes they can still get worse.

Khrushchev had a special interest in agriculture and often went to visit collective farms. After one such visit, his photograph appeared in the paper together with three cows. Khaim pointed out the picture to his wife.

"Here's our great leader," said Khaim, "the third from the left, visiting a collective farm in the Ukraine."

Khaimovich went to OVIR to request an exit visa to America.

"Comrade, I absolutely must go to America," he explained to the OVIR official. "You see, I have a brother there. He's deaf and unable to live without me any longer."

"In that case, Khaimovich, why don't you tell your brother to come and live with you here?" asked the official.

"Obviously you didn't understand me, comrade," said Khaimovich. "I said that my brother was deaf, not dumb."

Abram arrived in Israel. The next day, he met his first Israeli.

"How's the Soviet economy?" queried the Israeli.

"I can't complain," replied Abram.

"And how's the government there?" the Israeli inquired.

"I can't complain," Abram replied.

"And what do you think of the Israeli economy and government?" the Israeli asked.

"Here, I can complain," smiled Abram.

Three of history's leading military geniuses, seen in perspective in the USSR *after* the Six-Day War:

Kutuzov drew Napoleon's invading forces to Moscow, waited for the snow, and then drove them out of the country.

Stalin led the Nazis to Moscow, waited for the snow, and then drove them out.

Nasser led the Israelis to Sinai and is waiting for the snow to throw them out.

At a district party meeting.

"Khaimovich, why weren't you at the last party meeting?" inquired the official.

"If I had known it was the last, not only would I have come, but I'd have brought my entire family as well," he replied.

Soviet Jews define an optimist as someone who is insufficiently pessimistic!

It was a bitterly cold day, but still the line in front of the butcher shop continued to grow. After a few hours, the shop manager emerged from the store to make an announcement. "All the Jews on line must leave," he shouted.

A number of dejected people stepped out and, muttering to themselves, walked away. Several more hours passed with no movement in the line. The shop manager re-emerged. "Citizens, I am sorry to report, but there will be no meat available today," he announced.

One shivering person, still standing in line, turned to another and remarked, "Those damned Jews, lucky again."

Two Jews met on the street.

"Abram, where have you been?" inquired the first.

"In Berdichev—and you won't believe what I saw. Can you imagine, here it is 1987, and I saw Karl Marx riding on a tram!" exclaimed Abram.

"No kidding. That's amazing. Since when is there a tram in Berdichev?" asked his friend.

The KGB decided that the large-scale emigration of Jews to Israel would provide the perfect cover to infiltrate an agent into the small Jewish state.

"From now on, your name is Goldberg. Remember that," exhorted the KGB official to the agent in Moscow. "Make your way to Israel, settle down, learn the language, send us a simple post card with your address, and wait for Agent Petrov to contact you."

"But how will I know who he is?" asked the new agent.

"He'll use the following special code words: 'Don't water the flowers,'" replied the official.

Agent Goldberg arrived in Israel, found a home, began studying Hebrew, and awaited the contact. Months passed. Finally, Agent Petrov was instructed to find Goldberg and pass on instructions. Arriving in Israel, he made his way to the address Goldberg had given. But, lo and behold, in the building directory, there were three Goldbergs listed. Which was the right one? Goldberg had forgotten to indicate the apartment number.

Petrov decided he had no choice but to try his luck, so he pushed the intercom button for one of the Goldbergs.

"Who is it?" came the voice.

"Don't water the flowers," intoned Petrov.

"Wrong Goldberg," responded the voice. "You must want Goldberg the spy. He's in apartment 3C."

An American, an Englishman, and a Jew were arrested in the Soviet Union for participating in a demonstration. Brought to the court, the three were told by the judge that each would be released if he could respond to a single question.

"In what year did the Titanic sink?" the judge asked the American.

"1922," the American replied.

"That's correct. And now," turning to the Englishman, "how many people drowned in this terrible accident?" the judge asked.

"One thousand six hundred ninety-two," replied the Englishman.

"Excellent," said the judge.

And turning to the Jew, the judge said, "You there—can you name all the victims?"

An American was visiting a Ukrainian town.

"Why was the synagogue closed?" the American visitor inquired of a local official. "Perhaps it was because of your country's anti-Semitic policies."

"Not at all," replied the official. "It was simply because there wasn't a suitably qualified rabbi."

"But how could that be possible?" the American asked. "Do you mean to tell me you had no candidates for the job?"

"Actually, we did," said the official. "The first applicant had a diploma attesting to the fact that he was an ordained rabbi, but he wasn't a member of the Communist party. The second applicant was a member of the party, but he didn't have his diploma of ordination. And the third applicant had both party membership and his ordination, but there was one small problem — he was Jewish."

Rabinovich marched in the May Day parade carrying a sign that read: THANK YOU, COMRADE STALIN, FOR MY HAPPY CHILD-HOOD. Noticing this sign, a party official approached Rabinovich.

"Are you out of your mind, Rabinovich? You're so old that when you were a child, Stalin probably wasn't even born yet."

"That's precisely why I'm thanking him!" replied the elderly Jew.

*Category:* Women who have the greatest influence on men.

1. The German singer, Doris Baumgarten, thirty years old. When she sings, the capacity audience of 100 men remains spellbound.

2. The French striptease artist, Michelle Brio, eighteen years old. When she performs, no one in the standing-room-only crowd ever leaves.

3. The Jewish cleaning woman, Sarah Rappaport, seventy-two years old. When she locks the coat closet, not one of the 400 workers at

the brick factory can walk out of a lecture on "The Role of Tatar Women in the Construction of Communism in the Latvian Republic."

Abram and Sarah were at Moscow's airport waiting for the flight to Vienna and resettlement in the West. The plane was scheduled to leave at 2 P.M.

However, at 1:30 P.M. a voice came over the loudspeaker: "The Moscow–Vienna flight scheduled to leave at 2 P.M. has been postponed two hours in order to give priority to the departure of a Politburo delegation to the West."

At 3:30 P.M. the same voice came over the loudspeaker: "The Moscow–Vienna flight scheduled to leave at 4 P.M. has been postponed another two hours in order to give priority to the departure of a top trade union group to the West."

At 5:30 P.M. another announcement came: "The Moscow–Vienna flight scheduled to leave at 6 P.M. has been postponed another two hours in order to give priority to the departure of a Komsomol leadership delegation to the West."

At 7:30 P.M. a fourth announcement came: "The Moscow–Vienna flight scheduled to leave at 8 P.M. has been postponed another two hours in order to give priority to the departure of a KGB leadership delegation to the West."

Abram turned to Sarah and said, "Now that all those bastards have left, I think we're better off staying here. Come on, let's go home."

In the year 2075, in an Israeli school, a teacher was giving an oral exam.

"David, who was Leonid Brezhnev?" she asked.

Poor David couldn't for the life of him remember who this was.

"Aren't you ashamed of yourself, David?" said the teacher. "Leonid Brezhnev, you will remember, was the well-known protagonist of Soviet Jewish anecdotes in the last century."

Excerpts from the Israeli military code of conduct:

1. It is forbidden for the battlefield soldier to engage in any form of trade or commerce with the enemy in time of war.

2. When positioned in trenches, use your hands to shoot, not to talk.

3. Soldiers are not permitted to give unsolicited advice to generals in battlefield situations.

Khaimovich was asked about the principle laws of Communism.

He replied, "The first law is that everything can change. The second law is that there is no situation that cannot get still worse than it already is."

Khaim and his son were standing patiently in the long line to enter the Mausoleum in Moscow's Red Square to have a glimpse of Lenin's embalmed body.

"Papa, tell me about the story of Soviet power," said little Abie as the two inched their way toward the historic site.

"At first, we paid for Soviet power with our gold, our jewelry, and our house, then with our freedom, and even our lives during the Stalin era," replied the father.

Khaim and his son finally entered the Mausoleum, observing the order to be silent.

"Come on now," said the guard, motioning to Khaim and Abie. "Pay your respects and move on to the exit."

"And you see, Abie," whispered Khaim, "we're still paying."

Sarah and Khaim were discussing the news.

"Khaim, why does Brezhnev have to have more than one position?" asked Sarah, reading the newspaper. "He's the General Secretary of the Communist party and Chairman of the Presidium of the Supreme Soviet."

"I guess it's difficult for him to live on just one salary," Khaim replied.

Sarah arrived home from work carrying a copy of the party newspaper *Pravda*.

"What's new in the paper?" asked her husband.

"See for yourself," said Sarah, unwrapping the newspaper. "I managed to find some cabbage and a kilo of beets."

Abram was offered a choice. Either he could take a job as the person officially designated to wait for full Communism to arrive in the USSR, or he could take his chances and emigrate to the West.

"I've decided to stay hear and wait for Communism to arrive," he announced to a friend. "In the West, there is too much economic uncertainty, too much unemployment. Here, at least, with a job like that, not only is there job security for my lifetime, but it's secure for the lifetimes of my children, grandchildren, and great-grandchildren as well."

Khaim visited Moscow for the first time. He was given a city tour by his friend Abram.

"Look Khaim, that's Red Square and there's the Kremlin," said Abram, pointing out the historic sites.

"But Abram, why are there such high walls around the Kremlin?" asked Khaim.

"Because of the bandits," replied Abram.

"Which bandits—the ones outside or inside?" asked Khaim.

Khaim and Abram were in the zoo staring at a camel.

"Khaim, what kind of an animal is that?" asked Abram.

"It was a horse," said Khaim, sadness etched on his face. "But just look at what the damned Bolsheviks have done to the poor creature."

*Question:* Abram, how would you celebrate the sixtieth anniversary of the Bolshevik Revolution?

*Answer:* Sixty is the retirement age in our country, so I would happily go to Red Square, set a big table with lots of good food and drink, and have a party to send the entire Kremlin off on pension.

The good fairy came to Khaimovich and offered him the chance to make three wishes.

"I wish first that China would invade Poland," Khaimovich said.

"Your wish will be granted," replied the good fairy.

"My second wish is that China would invade Poland," Khaimovich said.

"Your wish will be granted," the fairy repeated.

"For my third wish, I wish that China would invade Poland," Khaimovich said again.

"Your wish will be granted, Khaimovich, but why would you make the same wish three times?" inquired the good fairy.

"So that China will invade Russia six times, three times on the way to Poland and three times on the way back," Khaimovich replied with glee.

Sarah and Khaim were discussing the news again.

"Sarah, have you read today's *Pravda*?" Khaim asked excitedly. "They're praising the Jews."

"At last!" Sarah exclaimed. "And what did they write?"

"They wrote," said Khaim, "that Soviet violinists are the best in the world."

During the Six-Day War, Dayan was sitting pensively, a sad look on his face.

"What's the matter, Moshe," asked an aide.

"I'm bored," replied Dayan.

"Well then, why don't we press forward as far as Odessa and occupy the southern Ukraine?" suggested the aide.

"Fine for today, but what will we do tomorrow?" sighed Dayan.

After a talk by a party lecturer, Khaimovich raised his hand to ask a question.

"Comrade, will we reach full Communism in forty years' time?" he asked.

"Undoubtedly," came the reply.

Khaimovich turned to his neighbor and whispered, "Fortunately, we won't be around then, but I sure do feel sorry for our children."

When the Communist party leader of Odessa died, Kogan followed the funeral cortege, sobbing uncontrollably.

"But why are you crying?" a friend asked Kogan. "Was he a relative?"

"No, that's precisely why I'm crying," Kogan sobbed. "How well I could have lived here in Odessa had I had such a person for a relative!"

David's mother was shocked to see her son's appearance.

"David, what happened to you?" she screamed. "There's blood on your shirt."

"Ivanov hit me," David replied.

"Didn't you react?" his mother asked.

"Of course, I did, Mama," said David. "I fell down, didn't I?"

Two Jews were walking down the street when they noticed two Russian men fast approaching them.

"Khaim," said one to the other, "what are we going to do? There are two of them, and we're all alone."

A meeting of Soviet humorists was called to discuss the disturbing fact that all current jokes seemed to deal with Jews. The humorists were exhorted to make jokes about other nationalities as well.

To set an example, a Jewish delegate was asked to improvise on the spot. He thought for a moment, then began. "Two Chinese are walking along the shores of the Yangtse River. One turns to the other and says: 'Listen, Khaim . . .'"

Petrov was sharing his thoughts with his friend Kogan.

"You know," began Petrov, "I thought that all Jews had a sense of humor, but I discovered it's not really true. Today, for example, I met a couple of Jews to whom I recounted a very funny joke. They only began to laugh seventeen seconds after I finished telling the story."

"Naturally," explained Kogan. "That's because they didn't think for a moment that someone with a name like Petrov could ever tell a funny joke."

A Russian and a Jew met on a bus.

"Listen Jew, why are you people so smart?" the Russian snarled.

"Huh?" replied the Jew.

"I want to know why you people are so smart," insisted the Russian. "What's your secret?"

"Our secret?" the Jew asked stupidly.

"Yeah, your secret. Don't you have some magic way that makes you smart?" the Russian demanded to know.

"Ah, now I see what you mean," smiled the Jew. "Well, in fact, if you must know, our secret is anchovies."

"Anchovies?" the Russian replied, dumbfounded.

"Sure," said the Jew, pulling out a can of anchovies from his shopping bag. "The whole secret is right here in this little can."

"How can I get some of the stuff?" the Russian asked.

"If you want," said the Jew, "I'll sell you this can right here. It'll cost you three rubles. Then you'll see how much smarter you'll be."

"Thanks, I'll take it," agreed the Russian.

The next day, by chance, the two met again.

"Hey Jew!" shouted the Russian. "That can you sold me for three rubles—I saw it in the shop for only twenty-three kopecks."

"You see, you're getting smarter already!" the Jew exclaimed.

A man went to a factory employment office looking for a job. During the interview, the personnel officer kept getting up from his desk, circling around the applicant, and staring at him from all angles. Finally, after several long moments of silence, he could contain himself no longer.

"Everything here in your application papers seems to be in order," the officer said, "but there's something in your appearance that tells me you may have some Jewish blood. Is that true?"

"Oh no, comrade," the applicant replied quickly. "It's just that I have an intelligent-looking face."

One of the greatest spectacles of the musical world was to have its premiere in Moscow — a symphonic orchestra composed exclusively of mice. And what a repertoire! Mozart, Beethoven, Bach.

Abram, an avid concertgoer, managed to get a ticket for the first night. When the concert ended, he rushed backstage to see the conductor, also a mouse.

"What a wonderful concert!" Abram told the conductor. "May I ask you a question?"

"Of course," the conductor replied graciously.

"Isn't your first violinist a Jew?" Abram asked in earnest.

Eight-year-old Ivan Ivanov had been taking violin lessons for a couple of years. Just before his first recital, in a concert of young performers, his parents thought of the ideal stage name: Abram Shapiro.

In the Jewish autonomous district of Birobidzhan, a teacher was conducting a class on the subject of atheism.

"Pupils, there is no God. I certainly hope that's clear. Is it?" she asked, looking around the room.

"Yes, teacher," the class responded in unison.

"To prove that there is no God, let's all look up at the sky and stick out our tongues," urged the teacher.

All the pupils except Abie dutifully complied.

"Abie, I noticed you didn't stick out your tongue. Why?" asked the teacher.

"Because if there is no God," reasoned Abie, "at whom am I sticking out my tongue? And if there is, I wouldn't want to spoil my relationship with Him."

*Question:* How many people live in Odessa?

*Answer:*    One-and-a-half million.

*Question:*   And how many Jews?

*Answer:*    What are you, deaf?

During World War II, medals were awarded to Soviet soldiers who participated in the liberation of Kiev from Nazi occupation. Now the Jews who emigrate to Israel, leaving behind badly needed apartments, are being awarded medals for the "second liberation of Kiev."

A Russian and a Jew were sitting next to each other on a bus.

"Abram, would you emigrate to Israel?" asked Ivan.

"Frankly speaking," replied Abram, "I'd love to go to Israel, but to whom could I entrust *this* country? By yourselves, you Russians would drink it to death."

Khaim walked into an Intourist travel agency office in Moscow.

"Young lady, tell me, please. How much does a round-trip ticket to the United States cost?" he inquired.

"Five hundred rubles," the agent replied.

"In that case, here's my money," said Khaim, handing over the cash.

The clerk counted the money. "But you've only given me two hundred fifty rubles," she said. "What about the rest?"

"That's all right," said Khaim. "I don't have the other half with me, so a one-way ticket will be sufficient."

Sign at Moscow's airport: "Would the Last One to Leave the Country Please Turn Off the Lights."

In the year 2000, Petukhov, general secretary of the Communist party of the Soviet Union, was asked how many Jews were left in the country.

"All 200 percent of our Soviet Jews have emigrated," announced the Soviet leader.

"What do you mean, 200 percent?" asked an astounded Politburo member.

"All 100 percent of the Jews plus an equal number who passed themselves off as Jews in order to leave."

Two ships crossed at sea, one carrying returning Soviet Jews from Israel to the USSR, the other, Jews emigrating from the USSR to Israel. As the two ships came abreast, the passengers on each ship stood on the deck and shouted to the others simultaneously: "Are you *meshugge*[4]? Where are you going? Go back if you know what's good for you."

With the so-called Jewish autonomous district of Birobidzhan in the Far East and Israel in the Near East, it's a big problem for Soviet Jews to decide whether to join near relatives in the Far East or far relatives in the Near East.

Kosygin's telephone rang.

"Hello," the official said.

"Kosygin?" the voice on the other end inquired. "This is Brezhnev. I wanted to tell you this Jewish joke I just heard. The Jews are saying that if our borders were open, the two of us would be the only ones left here."

---

[4]Crazy (Yiddish).

"No, no, Brezhnev," corrected Kosygin. "You've got the joke all wrong. If the borders were wide open, you'd be the only one left."

A Solomonic decision—Solomon Abramovich decided to leave the USSR. A wise decision, to be sure.

Khaim and Abram were unable to emigrate legally, so they devised a scheme for getting out. They were going to cross the border by dressing up as a cow.

As they approached the border zone in their four-legged outfit, Khaim, who was in the lead, whispered, "Oy, we're in for big trouble."

"Border guards?" asked Abram.

"No, a bull," Khaim whispered.

In the year 2010, Sidorov, the general secretary of the Soviet Communist party, announced that 102 percent of the Jewish population had emigrated in the twentieth century.

"How could it be 102 percent?" asked a journalist. "Were you also counting the unborn children of pregnant women?"

"No, we only counted those already born," the Soviet leader explained. "You see, some Jews emigrated and were foolish enough to return; but soon they got the idea and re-emigrated, this time for good."

The Odessa rabbi was asked the difference in voting behavior between stupid and smart Soviet Jews. He replied that stupid Jews vote with their hands, smart ones with their feet.

An announcement came over the loudspeaker at Moscow airport: "Attention, Attention. Those passengers with exit visas for Israel and tickets for Vienna are kindly requested to proceed to the Moscow--Gulag flight leaving from Gate 3 at 21:30. Thank you."

Abram Khaimovich emigrated to America. He was very anxious to share his experiences in the United States with his brother Izrail who remained in Odessa, particularly since Izrail's decision to leave the USSR depended so heavily on Abram's impressions.

The problem was how to convey his feelings without sounding too enthusiastic. Finally, he had an idea. This is the letter Abram sent to Izrail:

Dear Brother,

So what if we have a six-room apartment for the three of us. So what if we have a brand new car. So what if I have a high-paying job.

If you could just imagine, my dear brother, how difficult it is to adapt to such things.

Abram

Two Jews were standing and talking on one of Odessa's main streets. A third Jew approached and said, "I don't have the faintest idea of what the two of you are talking about, but I want you to know that you're both absolutely right—we Jews have to get out."

In the year 2000, a boy rushed home from school.

In a panting voice, he told his mother, "Mama, Mama, you'll never believe what I just saw on the street."

"What?"

"A real live Jew," said the boy, "and he said his name was Abram."

"You fool," said the mother, "that wasn't a Jew. That's a Russian who was unwilling to emigrate twenty-five years ago when he still had the chance."

The administrators of a collective farm were meeting to discuss the farm's financial problems.

"I think we need to raise more chickens," said one person. "This will help us to raise the capital we need."

"Excuse me, comrades, but isn't it true that Jews are emigrating from our country these days?" asked the bookkeeper.

"Yes, yes, but that has nothing to do with the business at hand," replied the chairman.

"I think that we need to raise more cows," suggested another. "That should give us more money."

"Excuse me, comrades, but isn't it true that the Jews have to pay 30 rubles per person just to submit their application to leave?" noted the bookkeeper.

"Well, maybe, but that really has nothing to do with our present concerns," insisted the chairman.

"I think we need to grow more alfalfa," proposed another. "Won't that bring in some cash?"

"Excuse me, comrades, but isn't it true that the Jews have to pay 500 rubles per person for the right to renounce their Soviet citizenship," interjected the bookkeeper.

"Stop interrupting us," shouted the others.

"I think we need to plant more wheat this year," said still another.

"Excuse me, comrades, but don't the Jews also have to pay 270 rubles per person for an exit visa?"

"And so what? Why do you keep pestering us with comments about these bloody Jews?" demanded the chairman.

"Because if it's true that the Jews are paying a total of 800 rubles per person, I think we'd be much better off raising Jews instead of chickens, cows, alfalfa, and wheat," countered the bookkeeper.

Refusenik Shneerson went to Moscow three times to try and get permission to emigrate, but he was unsuccessful each time.

"How much money have you spent on trips to Moscow?" asked Shneerson's friend, Rabinovich.

"About 500 rubles," replied the refusenik.

"Listen," said Rabinovich, "if you had used that money as a bribe to the Odessa OVIR instead of spending it to go to Moscow, you'd already be in Israel."

Abram had been silently listening to his friends as they discussed problems with OVIR. Suddenly his face brightened.

"Wow, will the last Jew to leave be lucky!" exclaimed Abram.

"Why?" his friends asked in unison.

"Because I'm sure," said Abram, "that as a token of gratitude for both the bribes and opportunities they've had to steal things from all the emigrants, the customs officials will *at least* pick up the travel expenses for the last departing Jew."

There are three kinds of Soviet Jews:

1. Those who have emigrated

2. Those who are about to emigrate

3. Those who are under the illusion they will remain in the USSR.

At the Israeli-Egyptian border, when Soviet military advisors in Egypt numbered in the thousands, the following exchange was observed.

An Israeli border soldier stared long and hard at the Russian soldier on the other side of the fence. Finally, the Russian couldn't stand being stared at any longer and shouted to the Israeli in Russian, "What's the matter with you? Haven't you ever seen a live Arab before?"

When Stalin's body was removed from the mausoleum on Red Square after he had fallen into official disfavor, the Kremlin couldn't find a place to put it. The Soviet ambassador to the United Nations was instructed to ask the other delegates if any country might be willing to take the body.

As it turned out, only the state of Israel was prepared to do so. After careful consideration, however, the Kremlin declined the offer on the grounds that the precedent of resurrection in the Holy Land made it too dangerous.

*Question:* How does an intelligent Soviet Jew speak to a stupid Soviet Jew?

*Answer:* Only by telephone from the West.

In 1937, during the height of Stalin's terror campaign, two inmates— a former colonel in the czarist army, and a Jewish Communist, an underground party member in czarist times—shared a prison cell.

"I don't understand," said the ex-colonel to his cellmate, "why it was necessary to make a revolution. Had you asked me, I would've gladly locked you up here without all this revolution business."

Kogan met his old friend Grinbaum a few years after the 1917 revolution.

"Give me some advice, Grinbaum. I've got 1,000 rubles hidden in my mattress and don't know what to do with them. I'm afraid to buy gold because the authorities might confiscate it."

"Buy government bonds," advised Grinbaum.

"But they say that the government will soon fall," said Kogan anxiously, "and then I'd lose my 1,000 rubles."

Grinbaum looked startled. "You mean to say you're not willing to lose your 1,000 rubles in return for the government's fall?"

Khaimovich, the old Bolshevik and participant in the Great October Revolution of 1917, was asked to recall his memories of Lenin to a group of young factory workers.

"It was on the eve of the Great October Revolution. I remember it like it was yesterday," Khaimovich sighed. "Lenin himself came to the factory and told the workers: 'Comrade workers, the power now lies in your hands. Hand it over, please.'"

During Stalin's reign of terror in the late 1930s, many of the leading military officers were killed. Khaimovich, seeing a newspaper photo of a Russian marshal bedecked with medals and ribbons, was heard to comment, "Such a young marshal and *so many medals*! One more, and he'll surely qualify as a target for the firing squad."

During the Yalta Conference in 1945, Stalin, Roosevelt, and Churchill decided to take a break from the work of discussing the projected post-War situation. Out of curiosity, Roosevelt and Stalin asked to see Churchill's watch.

On the back they found the following inscription: "To Winston Churchill, with fond remembrance, King George VI."

Churchill and Stalin then asked to see Roosevelt's watch. They found the following inscription: "To Franklin Roosevelt, from his friends and admirers in Congress."

Churchill and Roosevelt then asked to see Stalin's. On the back, they found the following inscription: "To Rabbi Moishe, from the Jews of the city of Warsaw."

At a meeting to celebrate the anniversary of the Great October Revolution, Khaimovich recalled his encounter with Lenin.

"It happened on one of those Saturdays when we were 'volunteered' to work for no additional pay. This small balding guy came up to me and started asking me silly questions; so I told him to get lost, and after he left, I turned to another worker and asked if he knew who that guy was. My co-worker told me it was Lenin. What could I say or do at that point?" sighed Khaimovich.

"Did you ever meet Lenin again?" someone asked.

"Never," replied Khaimovich, "but by the end of that day I had also had a chance to meet one of Lenin's closest friends, Dzherzhinski, the head of the secret police."

A Soviet competition was held to find the shortest Jewish joke about the country. First prize was awarded to Khaimovich on the basis of his one-word entry: "Communism."

Shapiro was brought before the court on a charge of having called the Soviet leaders a gang of bandits.

"But I was referring to America's political leaders," protested Shapiro.

"That's a lie," replied the judge. "When people mention a gang of bandits, they always have *our* leaders in mind."

Abramovich was late to the district meeting.

"May I have the floor, please?" asked Abramovich as he rushed into the meeting at party headquarters.

"Of course," replied the chairman.

"I would like to say," Abramovich gasped, trying to catch his breath, "that I agree wholeheartedly with the words of the previous speaker."

"But no one else has spoken yet," said the chairman. "*You're* the first, Abramovich."

"In that case, excuse me," Abramovich apologized. "I've only just arrived."

Khaimovich sought the help of a psychiatrist.

"Doctor, I have a three-way personality split," Khaimovich complained.

"Good heavens! What exactly do you mean?" asked the bewildered doctor.

"You see," Khaimovich explained, "I think one thing, say another, and do a third."

"I'm very sorry, Khaimovich," said the doctor sadly, "but we still have no cure for the effects of party membership."

Ivan was being considered for a party post but wasn't very happy at the prospect of being rejected. Fearing that something in his background might make him ineligible for the position, he wanted to avoid any possible embarrassment. But the party bosses insisted on reviewing his credentials.

"What's the matter, Ivan? Don't be afraid to share information with us," they urged.

"Take, for example, my grandfather. He served in the czarist army and then fought against the Bolsheviks," Ivan mumbled, shame written all over his face.

"So what!" said the bosses. "We're interested in *you*, not your grandfather."

"Yes, but my father went to America after the war," Ivan continued, his discomfort even more obvious.

"And don't we *all* make mistakes?" the officials soothed him.

"And I divorced my first wife," Ivan reluctantly admitted.

"But don't you make regular alimony payments?" the bosses inquired.

"Yes, but I've remarried. My new wife is a Jew," Ivan said, beginning to feel a little bolder.

"Big deal. We're a country where all nationalities enjoy equal status," intoned the investigator. "But you know, on second thought, the fact that your grandfather did serve in the czarist army and was anti-Bolshevik does make you ineligible for the post."

Khaimovich was summoned to the district party office.

"Khaimovich, if the party instructs you to work seven days a week at no extra pay, would you do so?" the party official asked.

"Unhesitatingly," came the reply.

"And if the party orders you to serve near the Chinese border, will you follow these orders?" the official inquired.

"Certainly, comrades," Khaimovich replied.

"And if the party tells you to move to a collective farm and to work in the fields day and night to help with the harvest, will you go?" the interrogation continued.

"Immediately," was the prompt response.

"And if the party orders you to sacrifice your life in its behalf, will you do so?" the official asked, concluding the interview.

"With pleasure," said Khaimovich. "With that kind of life, what would there be to live for anyway?"

Abramovich was expelled from the Soviet Communist party.

"Abramovich, why were you thrown out of the party?" asked a startled friend.

"Well, I was sitting at a meeting, and I fell asleep and had a dream. In the dream, I saw a big, beautiful mountain of butter with God standing on top. When I awoke, I felt the need to recount this dream to the others at the meeting."

After I finished, the chairman remarked, "You should know that God doesn't exist."

To this I replied, "And in this country butter *does?*"

At a Communist party congress, the speaker was exhorting the 6,000 delegates to be vigilant against the enemies of the USSR.

"Such adversaries *never sleep*; they are too busy plotting," the party chief warned.

A few minutes later, an announcement was made that there was a spy somewhere in the auditorium, and everyone was instructed to remain seated. KGB agents scampered all over the hall, but they were unable to find the enemy agent.

Khaimovich offered to assist them in their efforts. Within 15 minutes he was able to point with confidence to the likely culprit.

"Khaimovich, how did you manage that brilliant piece of detective work?" asked an admiring party official.

"It was easy," Khaimovich smiled. "He was the only delegate who looked wide awake enough to be plotting against anyone."

Private Abramovich distinguished himself in battle. As a result of his heroism, his commanding officer offered him the choice of a medal or 100 rubles.

"How much does the medal cost to make?" asked Abramovich.

"The medal only costs one ruble, but its symbolic value is incalculable," explained the commanding officer.

"In that case, I'll take the medal and 99 rubles," Abramovich decided.

At the draft board, a sad-looking Russian came out of the office into the waiting room.

"What happened?" asked those in the waiting room.

"They've drafted me into the submarine division for three years," sighed the Russian.

A few minutes later, an equally disappointed Ukrainian came out of the office into the waiting room.

"What happened?" asked the others.

"They made me sign up for three years in the infantry," the Ukrainian moaned.

Another few minutes passed before a very cheerful Jew emerged from the office.

"What happened?" asked the others.

"They've given me a permanent exemption," he sang out.

"On what grounds?" they demanded.

"Can you see that tree over there in the garden?" asked the Jew, pointing out the window.

"Yes," they replied.

"Well, I can't!" explained the Jew as he hurried to the exit.

In the army, the commanding officer was inspecting the men lined up for morning formation.

"Petrov, you're a proud-looking soldier. Big, strong, and healthy. Good lad. Ivanov, you, too, are a fine specimen, a superb example of our Soviet youth. Smirnov, that's the right idea, my boy. Good chap. Khaimovich, well, I suppose it's not really your fault. Semyonov, impressive broad-shouldered fellow you are. . . ."

In the army, once again.

"Soldier," called the officer, "you there, Ivanov, give me a two-digit number."

"Forty-seven, sir," replied the soldier.

"And why not seventy-four, huh? Give me another two-digit number," demanded the officer.

"Twelve, sir," was the reply.

"And why not twenty-one, huh?" demanded the officer.

"And you, Grinberg, give me a two-digit number," sneered the officer, turning to the only Jew in the group.

"Fifty-five, sir," Grinberg answered politely.

"And why not uh . . . uh . . . uh. Cut out those *damned Jewish jokes* of yours, Grinberg," the officer said, storming out of the barracks.

In 1942, during the Nazi occupation of western Russia, a Russian hid behind a tree and witnessed how the Germans and their local collaborators systematically slaughtered the local Jews.

He muttered to himself, "Those damned German bastards. Just look at what they're doing to *our* Jews. Just wait until we get to Germany. Then they'll see what we do to *their* Jews."

A few months after the 1917 revolution, Kogan saw his friend Shapiro on the street.

"Have you heard the news?" Kogan inquired. "Grinberg left for Argentina."

"So far?" Shapiro asked.

"Far from what?" was the puzzled reply.

During the Stalinist reign of terror, prisoners of every background were thrown together.

"Khaimovich, what did they lock you up for?" asked a cellmate.

"One evening in Odessa," Khaimovich explained, "I was in the company of a few people who were telling political jokes. I resolved to denounce them to the militia the very next morning."

"And what happened?" asked the other.

"The militia came that very same night!" Khaimovich sighed.

Khaim and his grandson Abie went to visit Lenin's body in the mausoleum at Red Square.

"Grandpa, who was Lenin?" the child asked innocently.

"Lenin was the man who freed your grandmother from her chains," Khaim replied.

"What chains?" the child persisted.

"Her gold and silver ones," Khaim said sadly.

Did you hear the story about the policeman and the old Jew?

"What's that you're reading?" barked the policeman at the frail old Jew.

"A book," came the terse reply.

"I can see it's a book, but what kind of book is it?" demanded the policeman.

"A Hebrew textbook," came the reply.

"And why, may I ask, are you reading it?" badgered the policeman.

"To learn Hebrew, so I'll be prepared when I go to heaven," the Jew replied with bravado.

"But what if you go to hell?" laughed the policeman cruelly.

"Then I'm already set. I speak Russian," the Jew replied.

During the great terror in the 1930s, Grinberg was sentenced to death by firing squad for sabotage.

"I hope," said the judge to Grinberg, "that this sentence will serve as a serious warning to you."

The grand leader of the Armenian people was lying on his deathbed. The elders of the community were summoned so that he could give them his last words of advice. They gathered at his side and pressed close not to miss a single word.

Feebly, he muttered, "Save the Jews."

The elders waited for other counsel, but, hearing nothing, went off to puzzle over the meaning of these unexpected words. Unable to make sense out of them, they decided to return to their leader in the hope of receiving some kind of explanation.

"Oh great leader of our people," said the spokesman, "explain to us what you mean by your earlier words, 'save the Jews.'"

"We have to save the Jews," murmured the leader, "because if they disappear, you can be sure that the Russians will be after *us* next."

New penalties for reckless driving:

1. A warning

2. Suspension of driver's license for one year

3. Revocation of license

4. Alteration of nationality in internal passport to "Jewish."

A Georgian and a Jew were sitting next to one another at a concert given by the internationally renowned violinist, David Oistrakh.

"Just look at it, would you," said the Jew to the Georgian. "Oistrakh, the son of our people, has been able to keep everyone in the audience in tears for the last hour."

"That's nothing," replied the Georgian. "Stalin, the son of our people, was able to keep everyone in tears for thirty years."

*Question:* What is happiness for a Russian?

*Answer:* To collect his paycheck, go out and buy a few bottles of vodka, and spend the rest of the money on a big dinner.

*Question:* What is happiness for a Ukrainian?

*Answer:* More or less the same as for a Russian.

*Question:* What is happiness for a Jew?

*Answer:* To hear a knock at his door at 4 A.M., find a KGB agent standing before him, and to be asked where Ivanov can be found.

*Question:* What happens when a person of Mongol nationality marries a Jew?

*Answer:* You get a Genghis Khan.

During Stalin's reign of terror, Khaimovich was called to police headquarters.

"Khaimovich, what was your address before the First World War?" asked the officer.

"110 Nevsky Prospect, St. Petersburg," Khaimovich replied.

"And what was it during the First World War?" the officer continued.

"110 Nevsky Prospect, Petrograd," Khaimovich said.

"And what is your present address?" the officer asked yet again.

"110 Nevsky Prospect, Leningrad," Khaimovich responded.

"And where would you like to live?" the officer concluded.

"To tell you the truth, I'm beginning to wonder whether I wouldn't be better off in St. Petersburg again," came the honest reply.

The ironies of history: In 1917, the Russians fought, the Gypsies stole, and the Jews traded. Today, it's just the reverse: The Russians steal, the Gypsies trade, and the Jews fight.

Abram was walking down Gorky Street in Moscow singing to himself, "Uhaaah, Uhaah, Uhaah. . . ." Khaim came along, heard this strange cacaphony, and asked Abram what it was supposed to be.

"Don't you recognize it?" asked an incredulous Abram. "I'm jamming the Voice of Israel broadcasts to myself."

In 1971, seven years after Khrushchev's ouster from office, the Odessa delegation to the twenty-fourth Congress of the Communist party of the Soviet Union asked that the deposed leader, always considered somewhat of a buffoon, be allowed to speak.

"Who needs him?" asked a delegate from Moscow.

"Don't be silly," replied an Odessa delegate. "The Jews say that it is better to go for two years without bread than one year without anecdotes."

President Jimmy Carter called Egyptian President Anwar Sadat.

"Anwar, I'll send you the arms you need. Just tell me what it is that your military requires," said the American leader.

"Hold on a second, Jimmy, while I call Moshe Dayan on the other phone and ask him what we need," Sadat replied.

During the height of the Stalinist reign of terror, there was a knock at the door of a communal apartment at 3 A.M. All the residents were so terrified that no one was willing to open the door. Finally, Abram mustered the courage. Facing him was not an agent of the secret police but a frightened neighbor.

"Hurry, hurry, there's a fire in the building," he shouted to Abram.

Abram ran through the apartment, knocked on all the doors, and shouted, "Hooray, hooray, it's only a fire."

While Brezhnev was attending a reception given in his honor during a visit to the United States, he needed a bathroom. Mr. Grinberg, the hotel manager, was fluent in Russian, and he was summoned to explain to Brezhnev where it was located.

"Go along the corridor, Mr. Brezhnev, and you'll see a door with the sign 'Ladies.' Don't go in there. Next door there is a sign that says 'Gentlemen.' In spite of what it says, you have my permission to enter."

Khaim met his friend David, a junior economist.

"How's life, David?" asked Khaim.

"Bad. I can't make ends meet," David complained.

"But only yesterday," said Khaim, "Brezhnev announced that things are going splendidly."

"Naturally he said that," countered David. "His business is far more profitable than mine."

Ivanov was called to the office of the factory director.

"Ivanov, you're an engineer. You earn a good salary and you live quite well, but I've received disturbing news that you're regularly receiving packages from Israel. From whom and why?" demanded the director.

"Let me explain," began Ivanov. "During the Nazi occupation, my mother hid two Jews. After the war, they went to Israel and, as a gesture of gratitude for what my mother did, they have been sending us monthly packages with clothing and other items."

"This is highly unusual, Ivanov, and most distressing. What, may I ask, do you plan to do about this situation?" asked the director.

"At the moment, I'm looking for another two Jews to hide," the engineer frankly replied.

Abram did nothing else at work except talk about the shortages of food, household goods, and quality clothing that he found every time he went shopping. Eventually, his complaining came to the attention of the KGB, where he was summoned for a meeting.

"If you know what's good for you," warned the KGB agent, "you'll stop talking about the shortages in our country. You know what we would have done had you said the same things in the 1930s, don't you? We would have shot you on the spot."

Abram rushed home to tell his wife Sarah what had happened. "Sarah, you'll never guess what I discovered today. Not only do we have shortages of food, household goods, and quality clothing; we're also out of bullets!" he said in amazement.

Khaimovich, the specialist in answering difficult questions, was approached by a perplexed friend.

"Tell me, Khaimovich, is it possible, as our leaders have said, to reach full Communism in this country?" the friend inquired.

"It is, indeed," Khaimovich replied. "It is possible to reach full Communism in this country; in that case, however, it is far better to live in another country."

Khaim and Abram were standing in front of the Israeli embassy in Moscow before diplomatic relations between the USSR and Israel were ruptured in 1967. Eyeing an embassy car, Khaim went over and suddenly slashed a tire.

"Khaim, why would you do such a thing, especially to an Israeli car?" his friend demanded to know.

"Ahhh!" exclaimed Khaim with a smile, "it's not the tire I wanted to cut; it's the Israeli air I wanted to breathe."

In the 1950s, after a meeting of the central committee of Rakah, the Israeli Communist party, Mikunis and other party leaders were returning home along a sunny Tel Aviv street. Oddly, they were all carrying open umbrellas.

"What do you need umbrellas for?" asked a passer-by. "Can't you see it's a beautiful day?"

"Maybe so," a party leader said, "but we just heard over the radio that it's now raining in Moscow."

During the Six-Day War.

Question: Why didn't the Israelis continue their advances and conquer the Soviet Union?

Answer:   Because in such a small country as Israel it would have been impossible to find enough military governors for the occupation.

Abram and Khaim were walking past the main entrance of KGB headquarters in Odessa. The sign on the front door read: ENTRANCE STRICTLY FORBIDDEN.

Abram turned to Khaim and remarked, "As if we would want to enter even if the sign weren't there!"

Grinblat worked as a museum guide in Berdichev.

"Ladies and gentlemen, in this room we have the skeleton of the leading Berdichev revolutionary, Comrade Petukhov."

"And whose skeleton is that little one next to it?" asked a visitor.

"That's the skeleton of Comrade Petukhov when he was ten years old," came the reply.

Abramson received his exit visa and held a party to say good-bye to all his friends.

"Khaimovich, what about you? Aren't you also planning to leave?" asked Abramson.

"No, I think the best thing to do is to stay right here," replied his friend.

"But why?" asked Abramson earnestly.

"Because when the war between Russia and America begins, we Russian POWs will live in paradise in American camps while the American POWs will live in hell in Soviet camps," was the ready answer.

In the Israeli Knesset.[5]

"The only way for us to solve our economic problems is to declare war on the United States or the Soviet Union," argued a member of the Knesset. "That way, when we lose, we'll be eligible to receive substantial assistance in building up our economy."

---

[5]Parliament.

"And what happens if we win?" interjected another Knesset member optimistically.

After Egypt's defeat in the Six-Day War, Nasser was seen in the Sinai Desert looking for the grave of Moses. The Egyptian leader was hoping to convince Moses to lead the second exodus of the Israelites from Egypt.

During the early 1970s, when Soviet-Egyptian relations were rapidly deteriorating, Brezhnev received a telegram: ISRAELI ARMY IS PREPARING WAR AGAINST EGYPT. SEND ARMS. SADAT. He didn't bother to reply.

The next day, Brezhnev received a second telegram: ISRAELI ARMY APPROACHING CAIRO. SEND ARMS. SADAT. The Soviet leader still did not reply.

On the third day, another telegram arrived at the Kremlin: ISRAELI ARMY HAS ENTERED CAIRO AND IS ROUNDING UP RESIDENTS. SEND ARMS. SADAT.

An answer from the Kremlin was soon forthcoming: CONGRATULATIONS. UNDER THE ISRAELIS, YOU EGYPTIANS WILL SOON LEARN HOW TO BECOME GOOD SOLDIERS. BREZHNEV.

Brezhnev and Begin met secretly and agreed to re-establish diplomatic relations and to build a lasting friendship between the two countries.

As they were about to take leave of one another, Begin said to Brezhnev, "Mr. General Secretary, I should like to say good-bye. I wish for Russia all that Russia wishes for Israel," Begin said as he boarded his flight back to Jerusalem.

"Dammit, Begin, do you want to start another cold war?" exclaimed Brezhnev.

Khaim, Abram, and Izya all decided to emigrate to Israel. Khaim managed to take some gold with him; Abram, some valuable jewelry; and Izya, nothing more than a few portraits of leading Soviet government figures. Of course, Khaim and Abram were astonished, but Izya simply explained that the portraits were "for memory's sake."

All three settled in Israel. Khaim and Abram quickly cashed in their valuables and squandered the money. They soon began to complain of difficult living conditions, but Izya seemed to be doing extremely well.

"Izya, how have you managed to achieve such success? After all, you only brought with you a few stupid portraits!" Khaim and Abram said.

"You two may call those portraits silly," said Izya, "but you should see the crowds that come every day to my shooting gallery and use those portraits as targets."

During the Six-Day War, Abramovich came to work at his factory in Kiev wearing crumpled pants and wrinkled shirts.

"Listen, Abramovich," said his boss, "why is it that you look like such a mess?"

"Let me explain," said Abramovich. "In the morning, I plug in the radio, and all I hear is about the Israeli-Zionist aggressors and the poor Arabs. In the evening, I come home, plug in the television, and all I hear is about the Israeli fascist imperialists. I can't stand it any more, so I absolutely refuse to plug in anything now, including my iron, for fear of what else I may hear about the Israelis."

In a Soviet classroom.

"Tell us, Petya, what do you know about the Dead Sea?" asked the geography teacher.

"The Dead Sea is a sea that used to be alive until it fell into the hands of the Zionist aggressors who set about destroying it. Thus the sea is now dead," the student replied.

The rabbi and the student met on the street near the university.

"Rabbi, what's the difference between dialectical materialism and historical materialism?" asked the student.

"Ay, you stupid fellow. No matter what the difference is, we'll all still be forced to emigrate," replied the sage.

The Israeli prime minister and his wife were having some marital difficulties, so she resolved to seek professional help. The psychologist immediately suggested that she change her makeup and use a more provocative perfume at night.

These ideas didn't prove in the least helpful, and she once again sought the help of the psychologist. This time he proposed that she change her wardrobe and pay particular attention to what she wore in the evening when the couple was alone at home.

That night she selected a sexy piece of black cloth that she casually wrapped around her neck, draped over one breast, and tied at the waist. She got into bed and waited for her husband to come home.

When he finally returned, he got undressed, put on his pajamas, pulled back the covers, took one look at his wife's outfit and said, "Thanks for reminding me, dear. I had completely forgotten that I promised to call Moshe Dayan this evening."

In Khrushchev's effort to liberalize the atmosphere of Soviet life after the harshness of thirty years of Stalin's rule, he decreed that all those in prisons would have their terms cut in half. The only problem was how to deal with those sentenced to life imprisonment.

Khrushchev puzzled over this dilemma, but to no avail. He then consulted all his advisers, but no one was able to offer a solution.

Finally, one aide suggested that Khrushchev consult the Odessa rabbi, a man well known for his wisdom. He called the cleric to the Kremlin and posed the problem to him.

The rabbi pondered the question for a few moments before offering a solution that Khrushchev readily accepted.

"It's really quite simple, Nikita Sergeevich.[6] Just make those who were sentenced to life imprisonment spend alternate days in prison for as long as they live," the rabbi suggested.

---

[6]Khrushchev's first name and patronymic.

The Berdichev rabbi was asked to explain the difference between an optimistic refusenik and pessimistic refusenik.

"An optimistic refusenik expects that he will be sent to Siberia," explained the rabbi. "A pessimistic refusenik also expects to be sent to Siberia—but only on foot."

Two friends meet.

"Khaim, how are you today?" asks one.

"Worse than yesterday, better than tomorrow," replies Khaim.

A customer entered an Odessa food shop.

"Do you have any butter?" the customer asked.

"No," replied the shop clerk.

"And eggs?" queried the shopper.

"No eggs either," came the reply.

"And when will you be getting butter and eggs, Khaim?" the customer asked.

"And how did you know that my name is Khaim?" demanded the clerk.

"I guessed," the customer replied.

"Well, in that case, try and guess when we'll be getting butter and eggs," Khaim suggested.

After Rabinovich's death, he was met by an angel who asked whether he preferred to settle in heaven or hell. Uncertain of the choice, he pressed the angel to show him both. In heaven, he saw nothing of particular interest; but hell offered card games, women, and wine. Not surprisingly, Rabinovich told the angel his choice was to live in hell; but when he went there to settle he found only fire, torture chambers, and chain gangs.

"But what happened?" protested Rabinovich to the angel. "Where is the first hell I saw?"

"Oh that," replied the angel, "that was the work of our propaganda department."

Dora was chatting with her neighbor, Sonya.

"My Khaim's wartime profession really helps us," boasted Dora. "He can tell two weeks in advance in which shop they'll be selling eggs."

"What did he do during the war?" asked Sonya.

"He was a scout," said Dora proudly.

In the 1950s, when consumer life was especially difficult, Doctor Khaimovich managed to cure a very ill woman. The woman, who happened to be extremely beautiful, was so grateful that she declared, "You've saved my life. Ask what you want of me, and it shall be yours."

"Make me a present of one night," suggested the doctor.

"It's yours," said the woman without a moment's hesitation.

"Go to the Central Department Store at midnight tonight, and get in line for the televisions that will be on sale tomorrow. At 8 A.M., my wife will come and relieve you."

An American delegation arrived in Moscow to visit a vacuum cleaner factory. They were shown the entire production process by the manager.

"According to our five-year plan, we should soon overtake the United States in the production of vacuum cleaners," proudly stated engineer Abramovich.

As the Americans were leaving the factory, they noticed a pile of brooms in the courtyard.

"What are those for?" one of the Americans asked.

"Oh, those are our spare parts," explained Grinberg.

Sarah bought a Soviet-made pot in an Odessa department store, but the next day she returned it to the store.

"Yesterday I bought this pot from you but didn't notice that there was a hole in it," she told the clerk. "Please give me another one."

"I'm sorry but we haven't any more pots," apologized the clerk. "Why don't you take this Soviet-made sieve instead—you can see for yourself that there isn't a single hole in it."

Khaimovich timidly approached the director of the housing section.

"Six months ago, I made a complaint that our toilet was clogged. Did you happen to lose the record of my complaint?" he asked.

"You're panicking unnecessarily, Comrade Khaimovich. We have complaints that sit here for years and years—and we've never lost any of them," the director reassured him.

It is the year 2000. Abram and Sarah are trying to recall political history.

"Abram, do you know a fellow by the name of B-B-Brezhnev? Who was he?" asked Sarah, perplexed.

"I don't know, Sarah, but why don't we have a look here in the encyclopedia," suggested Abram. "Let's see now . . . . Ben Gurion, Bonaparte, Brezhnev. Ah, here we are. 'Brezhnev, Lenoid. A small-time political tyrant in the age of Andrei Sakharov and Aleksandr Solzhenitsyn.'"

The Kremlin was so frightened by the Israeli advances in the Six-Day War that Brezhnev was reported to have threatened to bomb Berdi-chev unless the Israeli offensive came to a halt.

Khaimovich summoned the courage to invite a foreign tourist to his house.

"Tell me, Mr. Khaimovich, how do Jews in the USSR really live?" the visitor asked.

"There is no discrimination whatsoever against Jews in this magnificent country," Khaimovich responded loudly. "Now if you'll excuse me for a moment, I'll go and switch off the light and close the curtains."

"But why?" the tourist asked.

"First of all, we're economizing on electricity. And, second, safe as it may be for Jews in this country to talk to foreigners, it's still safer with the lights out and the curtains drawn," explained Khaimovich.

Averbukh returned home from the office. After dinner, he sat down to discuss the day's events with his wife.

"They installed a pay phone at our office," said Averbukh. "It's amazing how the phone resembles the office—it never works, but it still devours money avidly."

In the Moscow subway, a black man was reading a Yiddish newspaper.

"Excuse me, but why are you reading a Yiddish newspaper?" asked a startled Khaimovich.

"Because I'm a Jew," replied the black man.

"As if you didn't have enough *tzures*[7] being black!" sighed Khaimovich.

The teacher called in Abram's mother to discuss the boy's behavior in school.

"Can you imagine that your Abram had the nerve to say that he didn't write *War and Peace*? It just shows you what kind of bad pupil he is that he would even say such drivel," said the teacher.

"And maybe he really didn't write it?" replied Abram's mother.

The young boy was doing his homework.

"Papa, who was Karl Marx?" the lad asked.

---

[7]Troubles (Yiddish).

"An economist," Papa replied.

"You mean like our Aunt Sarah?" asked the child.

"Oh no. Aunt Sarah is a *senior* economist," explained Papa.

In 1956, after Khrushchev's famous denunciation of the Stalinist cult of personality, Khaimovich met his friend Abramovich on the street.

"Khaimovich, I hear that you were expelled from the Party," said Abramovich. "Is that true?"

"Yes," sighed Khaimovich, "I'm afraid it is."

"But why?" asked Abramovich.

"Well, I was asked to decorate our local social hall," explained Khaimovich. "I painted the hall, arranged the tables and chairs, and hung up pictures of Marx, Engels, Lenin, and Stalin. Then the district party chief came to inspect my work, saw the pictures hanging on the wall, and told me to get rid of the picture of the tyrant."

"So what's so bad about that?" asked Abramovich.

"I made the mistake of asking, 'Which one?'" sighed Khaimovich.

At Ben Gurion Airport in Israel, an immigration official was questioning new arrivals from the USSR.

"What was your profession in the USSR?" asked the official.

"I worked as a butcher,"[8] replied the first immigrant.

The official wrote down "Jew-thief" in the appropriate form, and turned to the next person in line.

---

[8]Butchers, able to save the best cuts of frequently scarce meat for favored customers, are often much better off than the average Soviet worker.

"And what was your job?" the official asked the second immigrant.

"I was an electrical engineer," he replied.

The official wrote down "Jew-pauper" and went on with his assignment.

"And yours?" he asked the third immigrant.

"I was a Communist party official," replied the man.

The official wrote down "Jew-jerk."

Isaac Abramovich Kogan was giving an exam to his pupils in a Berdichev school.

"Tell me, Ivanov, who was Genghis Khan?" the teacher asked.

"That's the first time I ever heard the name," replied the pupil.

"And Napoleon?" the teacher queried.

"Never met him in my life," came the reply.

"Julius Caeser?" asked the teacher expectantly.

"Couldn't tell you," mumbled the boy.

"Karl Marx?" persisted the teacher.

Petrov, another pupil in the class, couldn't stand it anymore.

"Isaac Abramovich," he shouted at the teacher, "why are you bothering poor Ivanov with all these names? You've got your circle of friends, and he's got his."

Shneerson arrived in Israel and promptly set about looking for a job. His Hebrew was good enough to be able to read the classified ads. One day, he saw an ad for a piano mover placed by a moving company. He made an appointment with the manager.

"I assume you're looking for a young, strong person to move pianos. I'm fifty-eight years old, I've had a hernia, and the doctor warned me not to try lifting more than five or ten pounds at a time," Shneerson stated firmly.

"So why did you come here?" asked the manager.

"To let you know that the job's not for me!" Shneerson said, as he made his way to the exit.

During the war of attrition between Egypt and Israel, the following occurred.

"Mohammed," shouted an Israeli soldier in the direction of the Egyptian trenches.

An Arab soldier stuck up his head, and the Israeli promptly shot him.

"Abdul," shouted the same Israeli soldier.

Another Arab soldier raised his head, and the Israeli promptly shot him, too.

"Mustapha," called out the Israeli soldier.

A third Arab soldier stood up, and the Israeli soldier picked him off as well. Angered, the Egyptian soldiers decided to try the same trick.

"Khaim," one yelled.

No response from the Israeli side.

"Khaim," the Egyptian soldier repeated.

"Who's calling him?" shouted the Israeli, safely hidden behind a rock.

"I am," said an Egyptian soldier, stepping out of the trench.

"That's number four," said the Israeli soldier, as he claimed his next victim of the day.

Abramovich was a well-trained Soviet guide who did his best to portray the glorious achievements of the Soviet Union. Work was quite routine until one day he ran up against an American tourist in a group he was showing around Moscow. The visitor seemed less interested in the high points of Soviet technological progress than in boasting about the wonders of American know-how.

"Hey, Mr. Abramovich, how long does it take you people to build that car over there?" asked the American, pointing to a Volga.

"About thirty minutes, I think," replied the guide.

"Ha! In the good old US of A, we can build that kind of car in less than six minutes," bragged the American.

The group then passed a new twenty-story apartment building.

"Hey, Mr. Abramovich, how long did it take you Commies to build that building?" persisted the braggart.

"Maybe six months," Abramovich replied, his frustration growing.

"Why, with unbeatable American technology, we can put up the same building in two months," the tourist proudly announced.

The next stop on the tour was the massive Lenin Stadium, the main site of the 1980 Olympic Games.

"Hey, Red, how long did that one take?" the American continued.

"I don't know," said Abramovich with a look of feigned surprise. "When I passed by yesterday, it wasn't even there."

A good question deserves a good answer.

"Khaimovich, why do you want to leave the Soviet Union?" the OVIR official asked.

"Because of the holidays," the Jew replied.

"What holidays?" the official asked.

"When I find fresh fruit, it's a holiday. When I find toilet paper, it's a holiday. When I find sausages, it's a holiday. . . ."

The trial took place only a few days after the Yom Kippur War in 1973. Citizen Ivanov was charged with having assaulted citizens Khaimovich and Abramovich.

"Citizen Ivanov, explain to this court what happened," said the judge.

Ivanov launched his convoluted defense. "I was watching the television news, and it was reported that war had broken out between the Arabs and Israel. Well, I said to myself, the Arabs will show the Israelis who's who this time. A few days later, I heard that the Israelis had taken the offensive. Well, I said to myself, the Arabs will soon stop them. Another few days passed, and I heard that the Israelis recaptured the area they had lost in the first days of fighting and were heading fast toward Damascus and Cairo. You can imagine how upset I was. I went out to the nearest bar and drank too much vodka. Then I stepped out into the street and saw these two guys (pointing to Khaimovich and Abramovich) coming at me. I said to myself: 'Time to fight. The Israelis are here already.'"

At the Moscow Zoo, a boy inadvertently stepped into the lion cage and was immediately set upon by the lion. A zoo attendant, witnessing the scene, rushed over and, in an act of great personal courage, entered the cage, warded off the lion, and rescued the child.

A journalist from *Pravda* happened to see the incident and went over to congratulate the attendant.

"That was a great act of courage on your part, comrade. I'd like to write a story on it for tomorrow's paper. Tell me, what's your name?" he asked eagerly.

"Abram Khaimovich," the zoo attendant whispered, a bit embarrassed by the attention.

Early the next morning, Khaimovich rushed out to buy *Pravda*. On the first page, in bold print, he saw the headline, CRUEL ZIONIST STEALS FOOD FROM POOR, HUNGRY ANIMAL.

Two Russians, Ivan and Petya, were walking along the street when they saw a Jewish-looking fellow approaching.

"Let's give that Jew a thrashing," Ivan said to Petya.

"But he looks very strong. He might hit us back," protested Petya.

"He wouldn't do that," said Ivan.

"Why not?" asked Petya.

"What could he possibly have against us?" Ivan replied.

To demonstrate his solidarity with the anti-Israel campaign in the USSR in 1967, Izrail Khaimovich went to the registration office and asked that his name be changed from Izrail to Egypt.

Ivan was six years old. One day he came home from school and told his mother that he wanted to marry another boy in his class. Ivan's mother thought this was simply normal childish behavior, but as he grew older, he continued to talk about marrying the other boy.

When his mother refused to consider the matter, Ivan responded by demanding an explanation, but his mother always said that he was too young to understand.

At the age of eighteen, Ivan, still anxious to marry the boy, insisted on knowing why his mother had such a negative attitude.

"You *cannot* marry him. It's as simple as that," the mother said.

"But why? Give me a reason," demanded Ivan.

"Well," said Ivan's mother, "what would the neighbors think of your marrying that fellow? After all, he's a Jew."

The wheels of bureaucracy barely turn.

"Why do you want to change your surname a second time, this time from Petrov to Ivanov?" asked the government official.

"So that when people will ask me what my name was before Ivanov, I can say Petrov instead of Abramovich," replied the Jew.

Khaimovich, the job-seeker, was called for an interview.

"Are you a member of the party?" asked the personnel officer.

"No," Khaimovich replied.

"And your wife?" the officer inquired.

"Also no," the job applicant said.

"And what is your nationality?" asked the interviewer.

"Jewish," Khaimovich said.

"And your wife's nationality?" continued the personnel officer.

"She's also Jewish," Khaimovich answered.

"Have you any relatives abroad?" the interrogation continued.

"Yes, my brother in Israel," replied Khaimovich.

"Anyone else?" persisted the officer.

"My wife's sister is in America," Khaimovich dutifully explained.

"Do you correspond with them?" the interviewer asked.

"Yes, with both of them," came the reply.

"Tell me, Comrade Khaimovich, nothing you've mentioned so far is in your favor. Isn't there anything positive in your life?" The personnel officer asked.

"Why yes. I've just received the result of the Wasserman test, and *it's* positive!" smiled Khaimovich proudly.

Khaim and Abram decided to convert to Russian Orthodoxy when they heard the rumors that there was soon to be a pogrom. They went to a nearby church, but at the last minute Abram got cold feet.

"Khaim, you go first and tell me what happens," Abram urged his friend.

Khaim went inside. When he emerged two hours later, Abram rushed up to him.

"Khaim, what did the priest say?" Abram asked anxiously.

"First of all, I'm not Khaim, I'm Ivan. And, second of all, go to hell, Jew-bastard," he replied angrily.

Kogan wanted to know what time it was.

"Hello, hello, is that the Office of Protection of State Property?"[9] Kogan inquired by phone.

"Yes," a voice responded.

"What time is it?" Kogan asked.

---

[9]The Soviet government's watchdog agency for many economy-related abuses, including theft, diversion of funds, etc.

"Noon," came the reply.

Later, in the day, Kogan called again.

"Hello, is that the Office of Protection of State Property?"

"Yes," replied the same voice.

"What time is it?" Kogan again inquired.

"3 P.M.," someone said.

Later still, Kogan went to the phone.

"Hello, Office of Protection of State Property? What time is it?" he asked yet again.

"Listen, stop disturbing us, will you? You're driving us crazy," someone screamed at Kogan.

"Hey, that's not fair," he protested. "You guys confiscated my gold watch yesterday. The least you can do now is tell me what time it is."

The Berdichev rabbi was asked by a visitor whether the Soviet people are optimists or pessimists.

"All Soviet people are optimists," confidently replied the rabbi.

"Why?" asked the guest.

"Because even the most pessimistic among them aren't as pessimistic as they should be," said the rabbi, shaking his head.

A factory advertised a vacancy for an electrical engineer. A Jew went to the personnel office to apply for the position.

"What's your nationality?" asked the personnel officer suspiciously.

"I'm Russian," answered the Jew."Here, have a look at my passport. You can see for yourself."

The personnel officer checked the passport and, sure enough, it indicated that the applicant was a Russian. Still, something told the personnel officer that the man was a Jew and, if so, that he shouldn't be hired. A clever idea came to him.

"I'm sorry, comrade, but we can't hire you because we need a Jew, not a Russian, to fill the vacancy," the personnel officer said smugly.

"A Jew? I'm your man. Ignore what's written in my passport. You know how those things aren't reliable. Of course, I'm really a Jew," the man protested.

"Prove it to me," said the officer. "Your passport says that you're a Russian."

The Jew unbuttoned his heavy winter coat, unbuckled his belt, unbuttoned his pants, and pulled down the zipper. He reached inside.

"Look at this," said the Jew, pulling out the bottom of his shirt. "Do you think anyone else could afford such a nice shirt?"

The intricacies of the Soviet legal system boggle the mind.

"I agree 100 percent with Soviet law and its interpretation," said Abram to Yankel. "There's only one point on which the government and I differ."

"What's that?" Yankel asked.

"What I think I earn honestly the government thinks I steal," Abram replied.

An encounter with a policeman can cause the bravest man to tremble, especially in the USSR.

"Those bandits, those bandits," shouted Abramovich in Red Square.

"Who are you talking about?" a policeman demanded to know.

"American bandits, of course," replied Abramovich. "And who did you think I had in mind?"

A Frenchman, a Russian, and a Jew were taken captive by a group of cannibals. This particular tribe believed that the human flesh of the captive tastes better if the final wish of the victim is fulfilled. Consequently, each of the three prisoners was asked what his last request was.

The Frenchman wanted a bottle of wine. The Russian asked for some vodka. The Jew asked that his hands be untied and that he be given a good kick in the buttocks. All three wishes were granted. The Frenchman drank the wine, the Russian enjoyed the vodka, and the Jew had his hands untied and was given a good kick.

As soon as the Jew recovered, he grabbed a pistol from the confiscated belongings and began shooting in the air. All the cannibals quickly scattered.

"Khaim, that was fantastic," said Pierre. "You saved our lives. But I don't understand why you needed the kick."

"I was afraid that if I wasn't kicked first, Ivan would have called me the aggressor," the Jew replied.

An East German, a West German, and a Jew were sitting on a plane. God came to them and gave each one the chance to make a wish.

"That there should only be a world without fascism," said the East German.

"That there should only be a world without Communism," said the West German.

"Excuse me, God, but will those two wishes be fulfilled?" asked the Jew.

"Yes, indeed," replied God.

"In that case, God, a cup of tea would be nice."

In an employment office, several Jews were sitting quietly, each absorbed in his own thoughts, as they waited to be interviewed. From the director's office, the secretary came out into the waiting room, assessed the situation, and announced, "It is not permitted to carry on political discussions in this office. If all of you persist in doing so, I will be compelled to call the police."

Maybe it was a case of "optical confusion."

"Hey, Jew, what time is it?" a stranger asked Abram.

Abram took off his watch, put it in his pants pocket, turned to the Russian, and said, "Can't you see for yourself?"

"But how can I see what time it is when your watch is in your pocket?" the Russian asked.

"The same way you could see through my pants and know I was a Jew!" exclaimed Abram.

Every day brings another problem to Soviet Jews.

"Sarah, while I was riding on the tram this morning, an anti-Semite wanted to hit me," Abram told his wife.

"How do you know, Abram?" she asked anxiously.

"Because if he hadn't wanted to hit me, then he surely wouldn't have hit me," answered Abram.

A Jew worked for a Russian.

"What do you do all day long?" a friend asked Abram.

"I sleep with the Russian's wife," Abram said nonchalantly.

"And what does the Russian do all day long?" the friend shot back.

"He sleeps with my wife," Abram answered without hesitation.

"Really?" asked the friend, not sure what to believe.

"Yeah," said the Jew with a wistful look. "I've made three children for him, and he's made three for me."

"What's wrong?" the friend said, hearing Abram's distress.

"I make Russians for him, and he makes Jew-bastards for me," sighed Abram.

Athletic competition is very intense in the USSR.

"The next race will be the 100-meter freestyle," announced the competition organizer. "Swimming in lane 1 will be Ivanov. In lane 2 will be Petrov. In lane 3 will be Fyodorov. And swimming in the marsh alongside the pool, in lane 4, will be Rabinovich."

Shapiro gave his son a parrot as a birthday present. The parrot immediately began to repeat, "The Jews are ruining Russia! The Jews are ruining Russia!"

Shapiro turned to his son and muttered, "You see, my son, here even the parrots are anti-Semitic."

Khaimovich packed a portrait of Lenin prior to emigrating.

"What is this?" demanded a Russian customs official.

"Not *what, who,*" responded Khaimovich. "It's a portrait of Lenin, our beloved leader."

Later, at Ben Gurion Airport in Tel Aviv, Khaimovich had to deal with Israeli customs.

"Who is this?" asked the Israeli customs official, holding up the picture from Khaimovich's suitcase.

"Not *who, what,*" replied Khaimovich. "Look at the valuable gold frame."

An international project was organized to research the effect of placing two men and one woman of the same nationality on a deserted island for one year. There were four groups of participants: the English, the French, the Russians, and Soviet Jews.

At the end of the year, the researchers went to visit the four groups on their respective islands.

On the English island, the researchers found three tents at some distance from one another. "We haven't met each other yet," explained one of the three. "There was no one here to introduce us."

On the French island, the researchers found two tents. In the first tent, they found a man and a woman. The man explained that he was having an affair with the other man's wife.

On the Russian island, the researchers found a large tent. Inside, they found two men sitting at a table playing dominoes, smoking, and drinking vodka. Pictures of Marx, Lenin, and Brezhnev decorated the walls. "This is our collective farm," they explained. "But where is the woman?" asked the researchers.

"Where she should be. Working in the fields," the two Russians replied.

On the Soviet Jewish island, the researchers found a small village with a synagogue, a school, and several shops. Children were playing in the streets.

"This is our town," a spokesman explained to the researchers.

There had only been three people to start with, but now there were at least a hundred. "Where did the others come from?" asked the researchers.

"We sent affidavits to our relatives in the USSR, and they came on the basis of family reunification," the Jews explained.

Abram Khaimovich married Olga Ivanovna, a non-Jew. Things being what they are in the USSR, when their first child was born, they registered her as Ivanovna, not Khaimovich.

Shortly after their daughter started attending school at the age of seven, the teacher came into the classroom with a very important announcement: "Class, tomorrow we're going to have a visit from an Arab delegation touring our country. You, Rabinovich, and you, Abramovich, and you, Ivanovna, from the mixed marriage, should all stay home from school tomorrow."

"Khaim, do you own a car?" Izya asked.

"Yes, I do," Khaim said.

"That's good. And a cooperative apartment?" Izya continued.

"Yes," came the reply.

"That's also good. And a *dacha?*"[10] the curious Izya persisted.

"Yes," said Khaim, somewhat annoyed.

"Wonderful, my friend. But, tell me, how much do you earn a month?" the nosey Izya went on.

"Eighty rubles," Khaim sighed.

"That's bad!" Izya responded.

Driving along Gorky Street in Moscow, Abram was flagged down by a policeman and was accused of having committed a traffic violation.

"Do you realize you've been speeding?" the officer asked.

"*Oy gevalt!*"[11] shrieked Abram.

"Excuse me, sir," said the policeman. "I apologize for having disturbed you. Foreign visitors are exempted from paying traffic fines."

Khaim was called to the Office of Protection of State Property.

"Where do you get all your money from?" he was asked.

"From the cupboard," was the unexpected reply.

"From the cupboard, huh? And how does the money get into the cupboard?" the government official continued.

"My wife puts it there," Khaim mumbled.

"Your wife puts it there? And where does your wife get the money from?" the official asked indignantly.

"From me," said Khaim.

---

[10]Country home (Russian).

[11]Oh, my goodness! (Yiddish).

"From you? And where do you get the money from?" shouted the official.

"I've already told you. From the cupboard," repeated Khaim.

Two strangers, both elderly Jews, were standing on the bus. One sighed loudly.

The other turned to him and said, "You're telling me!"

Abramovich, the blackmarketeer, was summoned to the police.

"Comrade Abramovich," the police official began, "your official salary is ninety rubles per month, but you own a cooperative apartment, a *dacha*, and a car. Your wife doesn't work, and you go on holiday twice a year to the Crimea. Perhaps you would like to explain how you are able to afford all this."

"Frankly speaking," said Abramovich with a sigh, "it's very difficult."

Khaimovich bought his son a parrot. When he arrived home, the parrot began to shout, "Kill the Jews! Save Russia!"

"Before going any further," said Khaimovich to the parrot, "I suggest you look at your own nose."

Cosmonaut Khaimovich has just been launched into space.

"Radio and television listeners in the Soviet Union, we are now in direct contact with our hero Khaimovich to see how he is doing," announced mission control. "Khaimovich, how do you feel up there? Your voice will be heard by everyone in the Soviet Union."

"For the first time in my life, I feel fine!" Khaimovich exclaimed.

The teacher was beginning the lesson.

"Children, how many legs does a four-legged horse have?" she asked the pupils. "Abie, you tell us."

"Oy, teacher, I should only have your troubles!" sighed the child.

Secretary of State Kissinger ran into the well-known Soviet journalist (and closet Jew) Valentin Zorin.

"Tell me, Valentin, are you a Jew?" asked Kissinger.

"Henry, I'm a Soviet," the journalist replied, somewhat dismayed.

"Yeah sure, Valentin, and I'm an American," shot back the veteran diplomat.

There was a loud knock at the door.

"Yes? Who is it?" asked the occupant.

"Does Khaimovich live here?" asked the unknown visitor.

"No," came the terse reply.

"But only yesterday I was assured that this is the apartment of Khaimovich. A friend of his gave me this address," the visitor persisted.

"Yes, yes, it's true, but he doesn't *live* here. He *suffers* here," moaned Khaimovich.

Abram went to Radio Moscow to apply for a job as a radio announcer. "I-I-I w-w-w-w-w-w-w-w-ant a-a-a-a-a j-j-j-j-j-ob a-a-a-s a-a-a-a s-s-s-s-s-p-p-p-eaker," Abram stammered.

"I'm afraid that we're not in a position to hire you because of your speech defect," replied the station manager.

"Y-y-y-y-y-ou a-a-a-a-n-t-t-t-i-S-S-S-S-S-emite," Abram struggled to reply.

Zeligman was asked to recount the most significant details of his life.

"I was born in Odessa in 1920," he began. "On the eighth day of my life, my chances of ever getting a good job in the Soviet Union were cut drastically," he said, completing his response abruptly.

Abram was racing alone in his car when he was flagged down by a policeman.

"Your license, citizen," the officer demanded.

"License, what license? We Jews don't have license to do anything here," protested Abram.

Khaim was filling out an application for a job.

1. Have you ever been abroad? *No*

2. Do you have any relatives abroad? *No*

3. Have you ever been charged with a felony? *No*

4. Nationality? *Yes*

Izya ran toward Abram, waving frantically to get his attention.

"Abram, did you hear?" he shouted as he reached his friend. "There may be a pogrom tomorrow."

"I've got nothing to worry about," said Abram calmly. "My passport says I'm Russian."

"Maybe so, Abram," replied Izya, "but the pogromchiks kill according to physiognomy, not passport."

A decree was issued that all Jews and left-handed hunchback bicycle mechanics had to pack their belongings and be prepared for deportation to Siberia within twenty-four hours. The Russian people were

puzzled. Why the left-handed hunchback bicycle mechanics also had
to prepare their things was simply beyond comprehension.

The opera *Eugene Onegin* was being performed on stage. Khaim was
among the spectators.

"Tell me, please, is Onegin a Jew?" Khaim asked his neighbor.

"No, he's not a Jew," came the reply in an annoyed tone of voice.
"Don't talk during the performance. Be quiet."

A few minutes passed.

"Tell me, what about that Tatyana who's in the opera? Is she
perhaps a Jew?" Khaim inquired further.

"No, no, she's not a Jew. Now stop bothering me," demanded the
same annoyed voice. "I want to listen to the opera."

A few more minutes passed.

"But what about that character Lensky? Maybe he's a Jew?"
Khaim persisted.

"Listen, I don't know, but if it'll make you happy and shut you up,
let's say that Lensky is a Jew. Okay?" asked the neighbor, his annoyance turning to anger.

"Okay? What do you mean okay?" demanded Khaim. "How can
it be okay when there is only one Jewish character in the opera, and
*he's* the one who gets killed?"

*Question:* What do Jews and endangered species in the USSR have in
common?

*Answer:* For the moment, neither can be killed.

Major Sidarov and Sergeant Siderkin were ordered to appear before their commanding officer to explain why they had beaten up Rabinovich on the tram.

"I was standing on the tram," began Major Sidarov, "when this Jewish-looking fellow got on, approached me, and started stepping on my foot. I looked at him but he didn't react. Then I pulled out my watch and counted sixty seconds. When the minute was up, he was still standing on my foot, so I hit him."

"And I was also on the tram," added Sergeant Siderkin. "I saw Major Sidarov standing there, and I saw the Jew get on. I saw the way the major glanced at him and then for a long time looked at his watch. I saw the way the major turned to the Jew and gave him a good wallop. So what did I do? I went over to the Jew and hit him too. Why? Because I also thought it was high time to hit a Jew."

Khaimovich and Abramovich met one another in the center of Moscow, on the corner of Mao Tse-Tung and Chou En-Lai Streets. Khaimovich turned to Abramovich and remarked, "I believe, Moishe, that things were a little better under the Russians."

Khrushchev asked the leader of one of the most primitive nations on earth how he had managed to resolve the Jewish question in his country.

"Easy," he said. "We had two Jews and ate both of them."

After the Second World War, Private Shapiro returned to the Ukrainian city of Vinnitsa only to find that the house in which he lived before the war had been destroyed by the Nazis. A friend suggested that he try to find temporary lodging.

"Please rent me a room or at least a few square feet in the hall so that I'll have a place to sleep," he asked an elderly landlady.

The old lady looked Shapiro up and down and closely studied his face. Something made her suspicious that he was a Jew.

"I suppose that you're one of those who doesn't believe in our God, right?" she asked him. "I happen to be a very religious Russian Orthodox."

Shapiro wasn't about to let the opportunity to find lodging go by so easily. "I believe in God," he responded.

"And what is the name of *your* God?" demanded the landlady.

"Jesus Christ," he lied.

The old lady was surprised but not fully convinced. "And what was the name of the mother of *your* God?" she asked.

"Mary," Shapiro said.

"And where was Jesus born?" she continued.

"In Bethlehem," Shapiro responded.

"Where?" the old woman pressed him.

"In the manger," Shapiro said without hesitating.

"Why?" the old woman further inquired.

"Because the anti-Semites didn't want to rent his parents an apartment," said Shapiro without blinking an eye.

A delegation of foreign dignitaries was being shown around Odessa by the Soviet leader himself when they came across a long line of people standing patiently in front of a fruit and vegetable shop. The leader was deeply embarrassed. The tour was not, of course, supposed to show the consumer ills of Soviet society. To the contrary, it was supposed to be another choreographed view of the carefully constructed Potemkin Villages—those mirages of progress and success—aimed at foreigners.

Stumbling for words to explain, the leader was miraculously rescued by Comrade Rabinovich, who stepped out of line, came up to the delegation, and explained, "Gentlemen, just imagine what a paradise we have here. We have already reached the final stage of Communism, and the magnanimous state now gives us all our food free of charge."

The foreign dignitaries were visibly impressed. The leader was so grateful to Comrade Rabinovich that he ordered the KGB to locate him and bring him to the Kremlin.

"Comrade Rabinovich, my dear friend. Tell me, is there anything I can do for you? Is there anything you need? Perhaps a car?" inquired the leader.

"No, thank you. I've already got a car," Rabinovich replied.

"Well, perhaps a *dacha*?" suggested the leader.

"That, too, I have," replied the Jew.

"But surely there must be something you need, no? Just ask and it's yours," promised the leader.

"Well, frankly, there is one favor you can do for me. Be so kind as to ask your economic watchdogs to keep far away from my business," Rabinovich said politely.

A group of resourceful Georgians managed to forge Soviet internal passports in order to list themselves as Jews. In this way they hoped to be eligible to apply for exit visas. The Soviet authorities discovered the plan and refused to allow them to emigrate. As punishment, they made the Georgians keep the Jewish nationality!

Abram and Khaim had both been refused exit visas several times. It consumed their thoughts every hour of the day.

"Abram, let's stop talking about emigration," said refusenik Khaim.

"Great idea. What should we talk about?" asked Abram, thinking that a respite might make him feel better.

"How about girls?" suggested Khaim.

"Good," Abram replied. "Let's talk about Sarah. I wonder if she resubmitted her exit application recently."

The Moscow–Leningrad train suddenly went off the tracks and into the heavy woods nearby before coming to a sudden halt.

"What's the meaning of this?" a passenger asked the train engineer.

"There was a Jew on the tracks," the engineer replied.

"So why didn't you just run him over?" demanded the passenger.

"I wanted to do just that; so when he saw the train coming and ran into the woods, I followed him," explained the embarrassed engineer.

An international comparative study was conducted, and the following results were announced:

- One Frenchman left on his own is a lover, two together are likely to have a duel, and three will start a bourgeois revolution.
- One Englishman alone is melancholic, two together will create a bird-watching society, and three will form a parliament.

- One Russian by himself is certain to drink, two together will have a fistfight, and three will form a Communist party cell.
- One Jew is likely the assistant manager of a shop, two together are sure to be relatives, and three are already forming a symphony orchestra.

A national food congress was organized in Moscow. Representatives of each of the Soviet nationalities were invited to attend and to bring something along. The Ukrainian representative brought a sumptuous cabbage *borscht*; the Uzbek, a rice-based, garlic-scented *ploff*; the Georgian, a lamb *shashlik*; the Russian, pancake-style *blini*; and the Jew, his family.

An argument was raging between an American, a Frenchman, a Russian, and a Jew over the nationality of Tarzan.

"Of course he was an American," asserted the American. "Who else would have such a physique and be able to swim so well?"

"No, no, Tarzan was a Frenchman," countered the Frenchman. "Only a Frenchman could have courted such a ravishing girl as Jane so successfully."

"You're both wrong," said the Russian. "Such a hairy, masculine chest could only belong to a Russian."

"What are you all talking about?" declared the Jew. "Tarzan must have been a Jew. Who else but a Jew would have been able to find a loincloth in the middle of the jungle?"

Khaim went to the Moscow Circus to look for a job. Jobs for Jews were hard to come by. The circus often traveled abroad, and Jews were not trusted to return.

"What are you able to do?" asked the manager.

"I can do somersaults," Khaim said.

"That's not enough. We need a person who can play the violin while performing somersaults, jumps, twists, and backward flips," the manager said, sending Khaim away.

Khaim went home and spent the next six months learning to play the violin and practicing acrobatics. Finally, feeling confident, he sought out the circus manager. "I think I'm your man now," proudly declared Khaim.

"Show me what you can do," the manager said skeptically.

Khaim went through his act with an array of acrobatics and violin playing.

"You're still not hired," announced the manager.

"But why?" asked the startled Khaimovich.

"A Heifetz you're not!" the manager declared.

Kogan and Petrov were comparing notes.

"Have there been any anti-Semitic incidents against employees in the bank you manage?" Kogan asked his friend Petrov.

"Absolutely none," replied the Russian. "We don't have a single Jew working for us, so how could we possibly have any such incidents?"

When Sarah graduated from the music conservatory, as a Jew, she was assigned to teach in a remote Siberian village while the other graduates were given plum big-city assignments.

"I can't go until I've discussed the matter with my husband and children," explained Sarah to the job placement director.

"But your papers show that you don't have either," the director countered.

"So what? I'll wait until I do," Sarah said cheerfully.

Khaim was sick and tired of living in a communal apartment. He spent all his free time looking for a proper place for his family and himself, but alas, to no avail. There were waiting lines years long. Preference was always given to party members. It was all a question of whom you knew—and Khaim knew no one. He wrote, without success, to the various state officials. Finally, out of desperation, he began to address his letters to "Vladimir Ilich Lenin, Moscow."

The letters came to the attention of the KGB who sent an agent to see Khaim.

"How would you like to be sent to the infamous Serbsky Psychiatric Institute? What's the matter with you? Don't you know that Lenin has been dead for fifty years?" the agent asked threateningly.

"Sure, sure," replied Khaim, "for me Lenin is dead, but you're the ones who have been trying to keep the guy alive all these years."

Khaimovich was summoned to his factory's employment office.

"Comrade, I'm afraid we must fire you. It has come to our attention that you're not a college graduate," the personnel director announced.

"But you're mistaken," protested Khaimovich. "I have a diploma to prove it."

A week later, Khaimovich was again summoned to the office. "Comrade, I'm afraid we must fire you because it seems that you're not a member of the Party," the director announced again.

"But I am," protested Khaimovich. "Here's my membership card to prove it."

Another week passed until Khaimovich was called to the office. "Comrade, you are to be fired because you're a Jew," the personnel director said, sure that Khaimovich was not going to be able to prove otherwise.

"A Jew? Me? You must be joking. Have a look at my passport. You can see for yourself that it lists my nationality as Russian," Khaimovich insisted.

A week later, Khaimovich was summoned to the office for the fourth time.

"Comrade, you are to be dismissed, effective this afternoon," the director said without further explanation.

"But why? Haven't I already told you that I'm a university graduate, a member of the party, and a Russian?" Khaimovich asked futilely.

"That may all be true," replied the personnel officer, "but, you see, we've just fired ten Jewish employees. To prove that the dismissal wasn't prompted by anti-Semitism, we now need to fire you."

Abram had a friend who was looking for a job. An opening occurred in Abram's factory, so he rushed to the personnel office to inquire on his friend's behalf. The personnel officer was suitably impressed with the friend's qualifications but told Abram that much would depend on the applicant's surname. The factory was not prepared to hire any more people with surnames ending in "berg," "baum," "ich," and other typically Jewish endings. Abram asked whether "ko" would be all right. The personnel officer, pleased with this typically Ukrainian ending, asked that Abram's friend come in the next day.

The friend arrived and began to fill out the application form: *Surname* – KOgan.

In the waiting room of the OVIR offices in Leningrad, the celebrated words of the well-known Soviet poet Mayakovsky appeared on the wall, presumably scribbled by an applicant for emigration to Israel: "I will sing the praises of my present homeland once, but of my future homeland, I will sing thy praises three times."

At the party meeting, an official was conducting a discussion on the construction of a Communist society.

"It's true that the Soviet people are being called on to make extraordinary sacrifices; but this is so our children will be able to enjoy all the fruits of those sacrifices," the official explained.

"But I don't have any children," interjected Khaimovich.

"Don't worry," responded the official. "If you don't have children, then maybe your children will have children."

Khaimovich's division was stationed near the Chinese border. Late one night the alarm sounded, and the soldiers quickly got dressed and ran outside.

"What's happening? What's the rush?" Kogan, the new arrival, asked Khaimovich, the veteran. "Where are we going?"

"To the border. In ten minutes, there will be a Chinese provocation," Khaimovich explained.

"And how can you possibly know?" Kogan asked, somewhat naively.

"And why else would we be going there?" Khaimovich asked, shrugging his shoulders.

In 1927, Khaimovich, Abramovich, and Shapiro all applied to join the Communist party. At the time, one's social origins played a major part in the party's decision to accept or not to accept a new member.

"Comrade Khaimovich, what did your parents do before the revolution?" asked the party secretary.

"They owned a small scrap metal business—not as big, of course, as the great November 7, 1917 Metal Combine that has been built in Odessa," the Jew replied. Khaimovich was promptly given his Party card.

"Comrade Abramovich, what did your parents do before the revolution?" asked the party secretary.

"They ran a small dress factory—not as big, of course, as the imposing Vladimir Ilich Lenin Clothing Factory that has recently been opened in Odessa," Abramovich replied. He, too, was promptly given his party card.

"Comrade Shapiro, what did your parents do before the revolution?" asked the party secretary.

"They ran a bordello—not as big, of course, as the bordello we now have in the entire country," Shapiro said in turn. He was not given his party card.

Khaimovich was expelled from the Communist party for no apparent reason. He protested the decision with letters of appeal to the district, and to national party offices, but to no avail. His claim of discrimination as a Jew was ignored. Khaimovich was desperate, so he decided, as a last resort, to appeal to Jewish public opinion abroad.

The reaction was so strong that Israel decided to invade the USSR. In a lightning attack led by the legendary Moshe Dayan, Israeli forces quickly conquered the Ukraine. Dayan summoned the leaders of the Jewish communities together.

"Now that we have come and are finally reunited, what can we do for you, our brothers and sisters?" the Israeli general asked in a voice quivering with emotion.

"Only one thing," said one of the participants. "Please try and arrange it so that Khaimovich is reinstated into the party."

After a political class in an army division, the following exchange took place.

"Comrade Major, I must report to you that the damned Jew Khaimovich asked an extremely provocative anti-Soviet question during our class today," the teacher informed his commanding officer.

"What did he ask?" the officer inquired.

"He asked: 'Can you tell us, please, how many republics there are in the Soviet Union?'" replied the instructor.

"And what did you answer?" the officer continued.

"It wasn't easy, but I managed to get out of it. I told the Jew-bastard to go screw himself," said the teacher proudly.

A few years after Trotsky went into exile abroad, Stalin received a telegram from him. The cable read: TO STALIN, MOSCOW. I ADMIT GUILT. YOU CAN CALL YOURSELF THE GENUINE SUCCESSOR OF OUR BELOVED LENIN. I OUGHT TO KEEP QUIET. TROTSKY.

Stalin was so happy that he took the first occasion to broadcast the telegram's text across nationwide radio. Shortly thereafter, Stalin received a letter from a certain Shapiro in Odessa who wrote that the Soviet leader had not read the telegram properly.

Stalin invited Shapiro to come to Moscow, arranged for a radio slot, and listened while Shapiro read the telegram to the nation: TO STALIN, MOSCOW. *I* ADMIT GUILT? *YOU* CAN CALL YOURSELF THE GENUINE SUCCESSOR OF OUR BELOVED LENIN? *I* OUGHT TO KEEP QUIET? TROTSKY.

In the early years after the revolution, the residents of Odessa had pitifully little to eat.

"I love ice cream," sighed Commissar Kogan. "When Communism comes, we all will be able to eat as much ice cream as we want."

"But I don't like ice cream," responded Blumenfeld.

"That's all right. We'll force you to eat it," Kogan replied.

Khaimovich wrote letter after letter to the local radio station, asking it to play the music of Soviet composers.

"But why, Khaimovich?" a friend asked. "It's awful stuff."

"That's just the point," explained Khaimovich. "When the music of Soviet composers is broadcast, all my neighbors shut off their radios. It's the *only* way I can get some rest in our communal apartment."

Abramovich went to the Mausoleum at Red Square shortly after the body of Stalin had been removed in the wake of Khrushchev's revelations about the dictator.

"Where's that fellow Stalin, the guy with the moustache?" he asked one of the guards.

"Oh, him. His next of kin came and took him away," replied the guard.

"And what about this other chap here, the smallish, balding one?" asked Abramovich, pointing to the embalmed figure of Lenin. "What is he, an orphan?"

In the immediate post-War period, at a time when food shortages were widespread, a visitor from Paris came to Odessa to see her old friend Roza.

"How nice it is to see you again!" Roza exclaimed. "You've traveled so far that I'll bet you'd love a cup of coffee, right?"

"With pleasure," the visitor agreed.

Roza went into the kitchen and searched everywhere, but couldn't find any coffee.

"Perhaps you'd rather have a cup of tea?" she suggested.

"I certainly wouldn't say no," the visitor said.

Roza called her son into the kitchen and gave him instructions to go look for tea. In the meantime, she began to boil water. An hour passed. Finally her son returned, unable to locate tea or anything else for that matter. Ashamed, Roza turned to her friend and said, "Since you've had such a long journey, maybe you'd rather have the hot water to soak your feet?"

In Odessa, a contemporary of the great nineteenth-century Russian poet Pushkin (1799–1837) was reportedly found. A special meeting was called at which he was to make a speech.

Pushkin's contemporary turned out to be Khaimovich, who began his talk, "In 1917 . . ."

The chairman interrupted him. "That's too far from the time of our great poet. Please start over again."

Khaimovich began a second time. "During the Great October Revolution of 1917 . . ."

Again he was interrupted by the chairman. "We all know about the revolution, Comrade Khaimovich. Now please talk to us about Pushkin."

But the members of the audience found the chairman's interruptions rude. "Let the old man speak! Stop interrupting Khaimovich!" they shouted.

And so Khaimovich was finally given the chance to speak. "In 1917, during the Great October Revolution, there was such chaos that I was given a new Soviet passport with—guess what—the wrong birthdate. Thus, I became a contemporary of Pushkin!"

Two friends met on the street.

"Moishe, I haven't seen you in years. What are you doing these days?" asked Khaim.

"I play in a gypsy orchestra, Khaim," Moishe replied.

"Tell me, are there many Jews in the orchestra?" Khaim inquired.

"Except for me and Abram, everyone is Jewish," Moishe explained.

Some people have all the bad luck.

"Oy, those damned anti-Semites," Abram complained to Khaim. "You won't believe this job of mine. I have to be at my job at 6 A.M., work nonstop until evening, endure the taunts of my boss and colleagues, and produce twice as much in order that they don't accuse me of slouching off. I tell you, Khaim, I just don't know how much more of this I can take."

"Abram, that's terrible. When did you begin this job?" Khaim asked sympathetically.

"I start tomorrow!" Abram replied.

An American tourist visiting Odessa for the first time was struck by the shortages of food, the dreariness of the city, and the sullen faces of the residents.

"Excuse me, please," he asked a passer-by, "but why is the situation here so bad?"

"To tell you the truth," Khaimovich replied, "it's because life, liberty, and the pursuit of happiness are not among our government's highest priorities."

In the 1950s, this was the typical scenario in the USSR:

"Oy," sighed Shapiro in the presence of his wife, "there is no meat, no milk, no margarine, no macaroni. If only there were no Malenkov, Mikoyan, or Molotov,[12] we could simply eliminate the letter 'm' from the alphabet."

---

[12]Georgi Malenkov (1902–1988), Anastas Mikoyan (1895–1978), and Vyacheslav Molotov (1890–1986) were leading Soviet officials for decades.

A delegation of Soviet women, just back from an official visit to a primitive country, reported to the central committee of the Soviet Communist party on the trip.

"First we traveled to Oola-Boola, the capital city," recounted the delegation's head. "We held a press conference at the airport and focused on the glorious achievements of Soviet women. Then the locals held a banquet in our honor, after which all the members of our delegation, except for Comrade Rose Kogan, were raped. The next day, we went to another city an hour away. Again, as soon as we arrived, we reported on the outstanding position of women in our Marxist-Leninist society. Then we were invited to a banquet and, guess what, we were all raped immediately after—all of us, that is, except for Comrade Rose Kogan."

"I have only one question," said the party's general secretary. "Why is it that Comrade Rose Kogan was the only one not to be raped on both occasions?"

"Because she wasn't interested," the delegation representative explained.

An American tourist visiting Odessa saw the World War II memorial to fallen soldiers of the Red Army. He couldn't help but take note of the number of Jewish surnames.

"I imagine that all of them died in battle," he commented to a local resident.

"No, as a matter of fact most were killed by Stalin at the end of the war without any investigation or trial," the Russian replied.

"But why was there no due process?" asked the puzzled foreigner.

"Who knows? Stalin told us that our soldiers were the victors and that the victors are never judged," the Russian explained matter-of-factly.

Definitions vary from one group to another.

*Pleasure for the Jews*: "Khaim, you've got a car, and so do I. Let's help David to buy one."

*Pleasure for the Georgians*: "Givi, I have a *dacha*, and you've got one. Let's help Lavrenti to buy one."

*Pleasure for the Russians*: "Petya, I was in a prison for five years, and you were in one for seven years. Let's denounce Ivan to the KGB and send him off to the camps for at least ten years."

Khaimovich, having recently arrived in Israel, hit upon a business idea. He would capitalize on the growing number of Soviet Jews living in the Jewish state by opening a Russian restaurant, called "Nostalgia," in Tel Aviv. To add a familiar touch he hired a doorman who was always sloppily dressed and drunk, and who was instructed to greet all the patrons thus: "Go to the devil, Jew-bastards. We don't need you here."

Grinberg, the stage manager, was preparing for a party meeting. Shortly before the session was to begin, he became frantic as he paced up and down with a picture of Brezhnev under his arm.

"What's the matter?" a friend inquired.

"I just don't know what to do with Brezhnev here. Should I hang him . . . or nail him to the wall?" he asked.

In New York, at a party held at Shapiro's home, the host was introducing fellow recent Soviet Jewish immigrants to an American friend.

"This is Mr. Goldberg. In the USSR he was a chief engineer at a large factory. Here he's a draftsman. And Mr. Abramovich was the director of an important institute. Now he works as a night security guard. And, oh yes, this is our dog Satko. In the Soviet Union he was a Great Dane, but here he's a fox terrier."

Statistics never lie, do they?

Ivan Ivanov, a key party official in Berdichev, confided to a friend, "A son has just been born to us, and he's a Jew."

"But how can that be?" the friend responded. "You and your wife are both Russian by nationality."

"That may be," Ivanov agreed, "but this is our third child and, according to local statistics, every third child born in Berdichev is a Jew."

When Stalin died, he ascended to heaven, where he met Moses and Jesus.

"Come, Stalin, and sit between us," the two said.

"No, I'm not worthy of such a position," Stalin replied.

"Not true," replied Moses. "You are greater than us. After all, I may have given people the law, and Jesus may have brought faith to many, but you alone, Stalin, managed to take away both the law and the faith."

An outstanding historian, Ivan Fyodorov, received the coveted Lenin Prize for two scholarly and definitive books printed within a month of each other—*American Imperialism: A Tool of Zionism* and *Zionism: A Tool of American Imperialism.*

There's a reason for everything.

"Teacher, why is it that caviar is never sold in our neighborhood stores?" the pupil asked.

"Because, Izya, it's a tasty but scarce commodity that our party leaders must keep for themselves. By eating it everyday, they are able to lead our country more wisely," the teacher explained.

During a visit to Israel, a tourist noticed three newly constructed monuments.

"To whom are they dedicated?" she asked the local guide.

"To saviors of the Jewish people," the guide replied.

"From the period of the Holocaust?" inquired the tourist.

"No, much more recently," the guide explained. "One is for the director of the Chernobyl power station, the second is for the personnel director at Chernobyl, and the third is for the Chernobyl party chief."

"But I don't understand what the connection is between them and the saving of Jewish lives," said the perplexed woman.

"It's simple," said the guide. "During the decade prior to the nuclear accident, the three were responsible for not having hired a single Jew at the nuclear facility."

Ivan met Abram on the street.

"Hey, Abram, look at the newspaper I bought," Ivan said.

"Why would you buy a newspaper in Yiddish if you don't know how to read the language?" asked the Jew.

"I'm going to use it as toilet paper," the Russian laughed mockingly.

"In that case, your *tukhes*[13] will be smarter than your brain," Abram replied as he walked away.

During the orchestra rehearsal, the conductor was reprimanding some of the musicians.

"Petrov, you're a half-note off. Komarenko, stop falling asleep. Saroyan, you're not joining in on time. Malashmili, are you playing those drums or caressing them? Now come on, let's do the piece over again with the damned Jews."

Khaim, unable to get an exit visa, decided to try and cross the border on his own. He managed to get about three steps inside the restricted border zone before powerful lights were turned on him, bells started ringing, and soldiers with their rifles at the ready came running toward him. An officer was the first to reach him.

"Stop! Don't move! Hands up!" the officer shouted. "Not a flicker of the eyelid! Keep still! Men, watch him carefully while I interrogate him. Now tell me, where do you think you were going?"

---

[13]Buttocks (Yiddish).

"Shhhh! Calm down. No need to get so excited and to worry yourself," said Khaim. "Relax. It seems as if no one will be going anywhere today."

A commission from Moscow was sent out to a rural district to investigate the reasons for which the collective farms were not fulfilling their plans. At each farm, the commission asked the manager how much grain the hens were being fed per day. The amounts, varying greatly, were duly recorded by the commission. Finally, the group went to the farm managed by Khaimovich.

"Comrade Khaimovich, how much grain do you feed your hens per day?" the commissioner asked.

Khaimovich was so afraid of giving the wrong answer that he hesitated a moment before exclaiming, "Well, you see, comrades, we give the hens cash and let them buy exactly what they need."

Abramovich arrived in Odessa from Kiev and wanted to call his friend, but he didn't have the number handy. So he went to a telephone center and asked to see the telephone directory.

"Sorry, but the city telephone directories have all been taken away by our glorious secret police," explained the clerk.

"But why?" Abramovich asked in dismay.

"They discovered that the directory was really a complete listing of Zionist agents in Odessa with full names, addresses, and phone numbers indicated for each. To disguise the list, addresses and phone numbers were also given for non-Jews," the clerk revealed.

You never know where anti-Semitism will rear its ugly head in the USSR.

"The director of the circus is unquestionably an anti-Semite," complained the midget Shapiro to a friend.

"Why do you say that?" the friend inquired.

"Because he wouldn't give me a job even though I'm at least a head taller than all the Russian midgets."

Consider the British perspective on anti-Semitism.

"Why is there no official anti-Semitism in England?" Kosygin asked a British journalist.

"Because we don't consider the Jews to be more clever than ourselves," replied the journalist.

Due to a heightening of tensions in the Middle East, the Soviet military command formed a special division of elite paratroopers and placed them on combat alert. The unit's motto was "Next year in Jerusalem!"

Different employers look for different credentials.

"Ivan Stepanovich," engineer Petrov told his boss, "you once told me that you needed a computer specialist for our institute. I have a friend, Kogan, who is a Ph.D. with more than fifty published works and many years of work experience. He is a long-time member of the party, was decorated for bravery several times in the war, was wounded twice, and is an ideological stalwart. The only problem is that sometimes he comes to work sloppily dressed."

"Oh, that makes no difference to me," replied Ivan Stepanovich breezily.

"I absolutely agree with you—it should make no difference," said Petrov.

"It makes no difference because even if he weren't sloppily dressed, we still wouldn't hire a fellow by the name of Kogan."

A Russian, a Ukrainian, and a Jew were each asked how much money they would want to agree to fly into outer space.

"One ruble twenty-two kopecks for a bottle of wine," said the Ukrainian.

"Three rubles sixty-two kopecks for a bottle of vodka," said the Russian.

"Two thousand rubles," said the Jew.

"Why so much?" the Jew was asked.

"A thousand for me and the other thousand for the person I'll find to fly in my place."

Khaimovich wasn't accepted for party membership because at the interview he insisted on answering every question factually. His wife asked him to try once more, but this time she urged him not to tell the whole truth. Another interview was arranged.

"Khaimovich, did you play the violin at the wedding of that ruthless anarchist Makhno during our Civil War? Did you actually play the violin at the wedding of a man who fought us Bolsheviks and wreaked so much havoc?" the membership chairman asked angrily.

"Yes, I did," Khaimovich said firmly.

"In that case, Khaimovich, we must again reject your application for admission to the party."

Khaimovich went home to tell his wife the news.

"But I begged you not to tell the whole truth," said his wife. "Why did you have to admit that you played at Makhno's wedding?"

"How could I lie?" Khaimovich said, shrugging his shoulders. "Most of the people interviewing me were dancing to my music at the wedding."

The Soviet educational system is a world unto itself.

"David, what did you learn in geography class today?" his father asked.

"We learned that we were supposed to unlearn everything we knew about China," replied the boy.

Brezhnev fell ill. A team of medical specialists was called in to examine the Soviet leader.

"Leonid Ilich, we have diagnosed the problem. It will be necessary to have an enema three times a day," advised Doctor Shapiro.

"What! Necessary for whom?" Brezhnev angrily shouted.

"Uh, uh, for me, Leonid Ilich," the doctor replied.

The Odessa rabbi was asked whether in the current period of severe religious persecution Odessa Jews still believed in God.

"Half the Jews here no longer believe in God," he replied. "The other half, those who still do, are even worse off than the first half," he sighed.

Izya met Abram on the street.

"Have you heard the news? Khaim got married!" Izya said happily.

"Did he do well for himself?" asked Abram.

"Splendidly," Izya replied. "Her apartment is located right in the center of Moscow."

As soon as Grinberg and his wife arrived in Rome on their way to the United States for permanent resettlement, they went out for a walk.

"You see, Sarah," said Grinberg to his wife, "the Soviet newspapers were right after all. They said that the capitalist countries suffer from chronic economic crises. Look at that building over there," he said, pointing to the Colosseum. "It's in even worse condition than our buildings in Odessa."

You won't find this in *Pravda*.

"Comrade Shapiro, we want to do an article on the life of the typical female Soviet citizen," explained the journalist. "How do you spend an average day?"

"I wake up at 5 A.M., prepare breakfast for my family, take the children to school, rush to my job, spend the whole day at work, rush to school to pick up the children and take them home, stand in line for hours to do the shopping, do the laundry and house cleaning, prepare dinner, wash the dishes, put the children to sleep, do some ironing for my husband, and go to sleep," she replied in one breath.

"And what do you do in your free time?" the journalist continued.

"Go to the bathroom," was the forthright reply.

Khaim went to the telephone center in Kiev to place a call to Zhmerinka.[14]

"I'm sorry, comrade, but you will have to wait at least four hours before the call can go through," explained the telephone operator.

"That's ridiculous," exclaimed Khaim. "Isn't there anywhere in the world I can call without having to wait so long?"

"I can give you New York in about one hour," the operator suggested.

"Fine," said Khaim.

One hour later, the connection was established.

"Khaimovich, your call to New York has been put through. Pick up the phone," the operator told him.

"Hello, New York?" said Khaim. "I'd like to make a call to Zhmerinka, please."

"Right away, sir," replied the New York operator.

Khaim worked as a salesman in a shoe shop. A customer entered the store.

---

[14]A heavily Jewish town in the Ukraine.

"Can I help you?" Khaim asked.

"I need a pair of shoes," said the customer.

"How about these?" said Khaim, pointing to a rather shoddy-looking Soviet-made pair.

"You must be joking," said the customer indignantly. "They're of such poor quality that I wouldn't even be able to make it home in them."

"Oh, don't worry about that," responded Khaim. "We can deliver them for you."

*Question:* What's a hundred-year war?

*Answer:*   A six-day war fought by non-Israelis.

Another Soviet-American encounter.

"Any Soviet citizen is more clever than your President Ford," boasted Grinberg to an American tourist.

"But how can you say such an absurd thing?" protested the foreigner.

"Easy. President Ford's not able to do two things at the same time, right?" challenged Grinberg.

"That's what they say," admitted the American.

"Well, any Soviet can," bragged the Russian. "Each of us is perfectly capable of simultaneously saying one thing and thinking another."

*A new Soviet decree*: All jokes invented by Jews are hereby declared to be against the law. In fact, the only exception to the decree is the best Jewish joke of all, the one created by Karl Marx.

Nostalgia waxed supreme at the local party meeting.

"Comrades, we are honored today to hear from Comrade Rabinovich, who will tell us about his life," the Odessa party chief announced to the rank-and-file. "Do you realize he was born in 1917? Comrade Rabinovich, we anxiously await your words."

"Thank you, Comrade Secretary," began the elderly Rabinovich. "I was born in 1917, the same year as our Soviet regime. I grew up with it, and now we've simultaneously lapsed into senility."

In a Moscow school.

"Teacher, what does the word *emigration* mean?" asked Ivan.

"It means moving or going away, Ivan. It is a punishment we have inflicted on the Zionists. Do you understand?" asked the teacher.

"Yes, teacher," Ivan replied.

"Good. In that case, please use the word *emigration* in a sentence," the teacher requested.

"Yesterday someone farted in our classroom. No one admitted to it. So the teacher punished the only Jew, Abram. Therefore, he emigrated to the hallway. The rest of us had to stay in the classroom to face the smell."

A KGB agent observed a young Jew, Khaim Lifshits, reading some strange-looking document near the Moscow synagogue.

"What's that?" the official asked suspiciously.

"It's the musical score to an opera," Khaim replied.

"Who wrote the opera?" the official persisted.

"Wagner," was the terse reply.

A few days later Lifshits was taken to KGB headquarters.

"We have arrested and interrogated three Wagners," a KGB agent advised Lifshits. "Each has confessed that the so-called music was actually a secret code for transmitting military information to the Americans. Now, Lifshits, admit that you were the conduit."

The Communist party leaders scheduled a rally.

"Remember and take pride in the fact that ours is a country of firsts," intoned the party official to the rank-and-file. "Ours was the first Marxist society, the first brotherhood of nationalities, and the first to launch a sputnik rocket," boomed the official to the cheering crowd. "Now, who among you wants to be part of our next first— sending manned space flights to Mars and Venus? Our country is looking for volunteers," the official announced.

"He forgot to mention one other first, Khaim," whispered Abram. "We're the first country in the world that gives its citizens the chance to visit Mars and Venus before they can visit France and Switzerland!"

At yet another rally, the crowd held on to every word.

"Comrades, I have the privilege of introducing our honored speaker this evening," the Odessa party chief declared to the thousands of workers packed into the congress hall. "Join me in welcoming our beloved leader, the General Secretary of our Communist party, Leonid Ilich Brezhnev."

After the thunderous applause had subsided, Brezhnev began to speak. "Dear friends, Zionists, and American imperialists!"

The delegates were stunned. The party chief quickly rushed over to Brezhnev's side and whispered something.

"Let me begin again," the Soviet leader announced. "Dear friends! Zionists and American imperialists are the worst enemies of our homeland. . . ."

Khaim and Abram met on the bus.

"Abram, come to our place this evening. It's been a long time since we've seen each other," pleaded Khaim.

"I can't, Khaim," apologized Abram. "Tomorrow at the university we have a big test on Marxism-Leninism, so I'll be busy all night with marxturbation."

After the results of the most recent general election were computed, the Soviet news agency reported that 99.99 percent of the voters had cast their ballots in favor of the party's candidates.

"Isn't it funny that in our daily lives we only seem to meet the 00.01 percent?" Shapiro commented to his wife.

Always fearful that others might suspect her loyalty because she was Jewish, Roza consistently aimed to be the top student in political ideology.

"Why was the Berlin Wall erected?" the teacher asked the students during the final examination.

Roza was first to raise her hand.

"Yes, Roza," the teacher said.

"Because the German Democratic Republic was compelled to protect itself," replied the eager student. "Without the wall, the residents of West Berlin would have rushed to the eastern sector, creating serious problems of housing and unemployment."

The Soviet official stirred the crowd to a feverish pitch.

"Comrades, the development of our Marxist-Leninist way of life is at stake," intoned the Soviet leader. "I'm prepared to give my blood, drop by drop, to the betterment of our society."

"My dear leader," shouted Shapiro from the back of the hall, "do us a favor and don't drag it out. Give it all at once!"

Khaim was walking down an Odessa street when he ran into his old friend Abram.

"Khaim," said Abram, looking down at his friend's feet, "it looks as if you've lost one shoe."

"Not at all," responded Khaim. "In fact, it's quite the opposite. I found one."

During the period of Stalin's Great Terror, Rabinovich was sentenced to death by firing squad.

"Do you have any last wishes?" the officer-in-charge routinely asked the condemned man.

"Just one," said Rabinovich earnestly. "I'd like my ashes scattered over Stalin's grave."

"But Rabinovich, our great leader isn't dead yet," said the exasperated officer.

"In that case, I can wait!" exclaimed Rabinovich.

In the Soviet Union there's always the danger of eavesdropping.

"Life just isn't worth living, and the leaders are jerks," Abram commented to Khaim.

Unfortunately for both, a militiaman overheard Abram's remark and ordered them both to appear in the police station later that day.

"But we weren't discussing our beloved homeland," protested Abram. "In fact, we were talking about life in Israel."

"Nonsense," replied the official. "Everyone knows where life isn't worth living and the leaders are jerks. Be at the police station this afternoon."

Humor is in the ear of the listener.

An Englishman laughs three times: when he hears a joke, when he understands it, and when he remembers it.

A German laughs twice: when he hears a joke and when he remembers it. He never understands it.

A Russian laughs only once: when he is rewarded for telling the KGB who told the joke.

A Jew *never* laughs: he already knew the joke.

A Soviet and an Israeli met by chance in Europe and began to compare notes.

"In Israel, we have a real miracle," boasted the Israeli. "It's called the Dead Sea. No matter how hard you try, you can't drown. People from as far away as the United States, Canada, and Australia come to see it."

"That's nothing," retorted the Soviet. "In our country we have the Dead Land. No matter how hard you try, you can't reap a harvest. People from as far away as the United States, Canada, and Australia send us grain."

Gorbachev decided to quietly visit the homes of some typical Soviet citizens to gain a better understanding of their everyday life. For starters, he knocked on the door of a second-floor apartment in one of Moscow's newly constructed suburbs.

"May I come in and speak with your parents?" Gorbachev asked.

"Certainly," replied the teenager, who obviously did not recognize the new Soviet leader. "Who may I say would like to see them?"

"Tell them it's the person who is responsible for providing them with all these luxurious amenities," said Gorbachev, pointing his finger at the television, shortwave radio, stereo, and tape recorder prominently displayed in the living room wall unit.

"Mama, Papa," the girl excitedly shouted. "Uncle Khaim from Haifa is here to see you."

At the Red Dawn collective farm, a problem had developed. Every night, usually around 2 or 3 A.M., Rabinovich, a long-standing member of the farm, could be seen pushing a wheelbarrow from the farm in the direction of the nearest town. The lone sentry on duty reported this suspicious behavior to the farm's manager.

Rather than confront Rabinovich immediately, the decision was made to watch his every movement. Night after night, Rabinovich could be observed repeating the same pattern. Clearly, the manager concluded, the man must be stealing something from the farm, but what? Thorough checks of every item small enough to be concealed in a wheelbarrow had uncovered nothing.

At wit's end, the manager decided to call in Rabinovich. "Comrade Rabinovich, we know you're stealing something from the farm; but, frankly, we've wasted a lot of time and haven't been able to figure out what. I give you my word—we won't punish you as long as you tell me what it is you're taking," said the manager.

"Wheelbarrows," replied Rabinovich.

A journalist confronted General Secretary Gorbachev.

"Why is the Soviet Union now refusing so many Jews the right to emigrate on the grounds of state security? Can it really be possible that hundreds of thousands of Jews, old and young alike, have really had access to state secrets?" the foreign journalist asked Gorbachev.

"Of course. Thanks to our campaign of *glasnost*[15] everyone in the country—Jews and others—now knows exactly what's going on. That makes them all holders of state secrets, doesn't it?"

Shortly after the Soviet press offered the first hints that relations with Mao Tse-Tung's China were strained, Khaimovich and his wife entered a neighborhood grocery store.

"I would like a one-kilo bag of rice, please," he asked the clerk.

---

[15]Openness (Russian).

"We have no rice," she replied, pointing in the direction of the empty shelves behind her.

"Oy, things with China must be even worse than I thought," muttered Khaimovich.

Just prior to leaving his native Moscow for a new life in Israel, Shapiro advised his remaining relatives to be careful in their correspondence with him.

"Remember not to write me about the actual situation here. You and I both know how dangerous that would be," he warned. "Instead, send me photographs. If things are good for you, be standing. If things are bad, be seated."

A month later, Shapiro, now a resident in an immigrant absorption center near Jerusalem, received his first envelope from Moscow. Inside was a picture of his relatives. They were all lying down!

Six-year-old Abie was lost in downtown Odessa until a policeman approached.

"Tell me your address, little boy," the policeman said.

"I don't know it," Abie nervously replied.

"Don't worry," the policeman assured him. "We'll broadcast some information about you on the radio. Your parents will hear it and come get you."

"In that case, be sure to use the Voice of America. That's the only station they listen to," suggested Abie.

# PART II

## General Political Humor

*Question from Armenian Radio*[1]:  What's the difference between a
   Soviet optimist and pessimist?

*Answer:*   An optimist studies English, a pessimist, Chinese.

Three dogs, an American, an English, and a Russian, met in Austria
after all had fled their native lands.
   "And why did you leave?" the American dog was asked.
   "Because of crime and unemployment," he noted.
   "And what about you?" the English dog was asked.
   "Because Britain is fast going downhill," he replied.
   "And you?" the Russian dog was asked.
   "Well, everything was basically okay for me in Russia. I had
enough to eat, a job, and a roof over my head; but the problem was
that every once in a while a dog feels the need to bark," he explained.

---

[1]A fictitious radio station that has been the vehicle for much underground political
humor in the USSR.

161

As Gorbachev's anti-alcoholism campaign intensified, it became increasingly difficult to purchase once-ubiquitous vodka. So it was that two Russians, forced to wait in a long line, began to complain about the Soviet leader's attitude.

"You know," said one, "the problem with our leader is that he must be a teetotaler."

"Maybe so," replied the other, "but look at the bright side. He could have been celibate."

The USSR is proud of its sophisticated technology.

"Ivan, did you hear about the newly designed telephone that links local party workers with the Kremlin?" Petrov asked.

"No. What's new about it?" Ivan inquired, curiously.

"It has an earpiece, but no mouthpiece," explained Petrov.

*Question from Armenian Radio:* Is it possible to build Communism in any country?

*Answer:*   Yes, it is, but who the hell would want to do it?

When Madame Furtseva, the late minister of culture, came to Paris for an official visit, French President Pompidou reportedly commented: "I saw the minister of culture, but I didn't see the culture of the minister."

*Question from Armenian Radio:* Who were the first Communists in history?

*Answer:* Adam and Eve. They walked around naked, had one apple between them, and thought they lived in paradise.

Shortly after Gorbachev's anti-alcoholism campaign got into full swing, the Soviet leader returned to his apartment from his Kremlin office and knocked on the door of his wife Raisa's bedroom.

"Hurry up and get out of here," Raisa whispered to Foreign Minister Shevardnadze, who was with her in bed.

"But why," protested Shevardnadze, "we're not drinking."

*Question:* Why did Brezhnev always kiss Kosygin on both cheeks and then shake the hands of all the members of the Politburo immediately upon returning from each trip abroad?

*Answer:* The first time he kisses Kosygin he is actually whispering in his ear: "Am I still leader of the country?" The second kiss gives Kosygin the chance to respond. The handshake with each Politburo member is actually a thank you from Brezhnev for not having deposed him during his absence.

A new bookstore was opened in Moscow. When the manager displayed a copy of Dostoyevsky's *The Idiot* with Brezhnev's picture on the cover, he was promptly summoned to the police and warned to put an end to such disrespectful behavior.

A few days later, however, the manager was again called to the police, this time for displaying a copy of Turgenev's *The Parasites* with a picture of Brezhnev's family on the cover. He was advised that any further such incidents would lead to his immediate arrest and imprisonment.

A week passed before the manager was taken into custody for a third time. The charge? Displaying a copy of *Ali Baba and the Forty Thieves* with a picture of Brezhnev and the members of the Politburo on the cover.

When Ivan arrived late for the trade union meeting, he was surprised to discover no one sitting in the audience; instead, everyone was on the stage behind the speaker.

"What happened?" Ivan asked the cloakroom attendant.

"The chairman of our local decided to appoint all the members to the presidium," he explained. "Then he could seat them on the stage. That way they couldn't walk out before the end of the meeting, as they did when they were just plain rank-and-file."

Every month a meeting of the party was scheduled.

"Is everything clear? Are there any questions?" the party boss asked the members gathered to listen to a speech on recent party policy.

"I have a question," said Ivan. "Where is the butter? Why is there no butter in the shops?"

"Comrade, I can't answer that question now, but I'll explain the reason at our next meeting," promised the party boss.

One month later, the next meeting took place. "Comrades," concluded the party boss, "I trust I've explained our party's foreign and domestic accomplishments to your satisfaction. Are there any questions?"

"I have one," said Ivan. "Where's the butter?"

"Comrade, I'm afraid I can't answer that question at the moment, but I'll most certainly give you an answer at our next meeting," the party boss promised once again.

At the next meeting, Ivan wasn't there. "Comrades," intoned the party boss, "I've concluded my remarks on the successes of our great party. Are there any questions?"

"I have one," came a voice from the eighth row. "First the butter disappeared. Can it be that Ivan has also?"

Ivanov submitted a doctoral dissertation to the academic review board. The subject: "Soviet Progressive Paralysis, the Most Progressive in the World."

*Question from Armenian Radio:* Is it possible to build Communism in the Republic of Armenia?

*Answer:* Yes, but it would be better to do it in the Republic of Georgia.

Ivanov was standing in a very long line for vodka.

"We have General Secretary Gorbachev to thank for such a long line," one of Ivanov's neighbors in line muttered. "He's making the stuff very scarce."

"I can't endure this any more," Ivanov said, walking away. "I'm going to get my rifle and kill Gorbachev."

Two hours later Ivanov returned to the line. "What happened?" the others asked.

"I decided to get back in this line. It's shorter than the line to kill Gorbachev."

The *Moscow Evening News* advertised a contest for the best political joke. First prize was ten years in prison; second prize, five years; third prize, three years; and there were six honorable mentions of one year each.

In the Soviet Union, no one does anything without written instructions. Thus, when there was a knock at Brezhnev's bedroom door late one night, the Soviet leader got up, put on his robe and slippers, and walked over to a file box of instructions.

Looking under the letter "k," he found the appropriate instruction card for "Knock on the Door" and pulled it out. Reaching the door, he slowly read out in a loud voice: "Who . . . is . . . it?"

Chinese tactics to win a war against the Soviet Union: As soon as the war starts, let the Russians capture one million Chinese soldiers. On the second day, let them take another two million. On the third day, give them ten million more. By the fifth day, they should have taken as many as twenty million men.

Keep up the same tactics while the Russians try to house and feed all the prisoners. Then, at the end of the second week, Mao will phone Brezhnev and ask if he's ready to surrender.

*Question:* What is the principal difference between capitalism and Communism?

*Answer:* Under capitalism, shopkeepers put up signs that read "We Have Fresh Milk" or "Eggs on Sale." Under Communism, the shop managers put up signs that read: "It is Hereby Decreed That There Will Be No Need for Milk or Eggs Today."

The harvest in China was so bad that Mao was forced to cable Khrushchev: HUNGER RAMPANT. SEND WHEAT IMMEDI-ATELY. A few hours later, Mao received a cable from the Soviet leader: OUR OWN WHEAT SITUATION PRECARIOUS. SUG-GEST YOU TIGHTEN BELTS. Mao quickly replied: SEND BELTS.

During Brezhnev's round of talks with Nixon in the White House, he noticed a red telephone on Nixon's desk and asked its purpose.

"Ah, that. It's the latest example of America's capacity for technological innovation. I can call hell on that phone. If you'd like, I'll show you," Nixon offered.

"Yes, yes," replied Brezhnev enthusiastically.

Nixon picked up the receiver. "Operator, connect me with hell," he said.

"Yes, sir," said the operator. "Please deposit fifty dollars in coins."

Nixon deposited the money and was connected with the devil. Brezhnev was so impressed by this phone that, upon his return to Moscow, he ordered his engineers to come up with a similar one within ten days. On the tenth day, a red phone was installed in Brezhnev's office. Surrounded by journalists and party officials, he picked up the receiver.

"Operator," he said, "Connect me with hell."

"Yes, comrade," the operator replied. "Please deposit three kopecks."

"Three kopecks!" shouted Brezhnev. "That's less than five American cents. But in Washington the same call costs fifty dollars."

"Yes," replied the operator, "but there, Comrade Brezhnev, it was a long-distance call; here it's local."

*Question from Armenian Radio:* What is capitalism?

*Answer:*   The exploitation of man by man.

*Question:* And what is Communism?

*Answer:*   The reverse.

General Secretary Brezhnev went to Moscow's airport to meet the arriving President Nixon. After a brief welcoming ceremony, the two leaders entered the waiting limousine and proceeded in the direction of the Kremlin.

To insure that he would make a favorable impression, Brezhnev had ordered that all the houses along the route should be repaired and painted, all the shop windows should be crammed with goods, and that, apart from normal pedestrian traffic, people should not be encouraged to line the streets.

All was going well for Brezhnev until the limousine passed a man urinating in the middle of the street. Nixon remarked that such an incident hadn't occurred in Washington for decades. The Soviet leader was so embarrassed that he ordered the culprit arrested and imprisoned.

When Brezhnev subsequently visited Nixon in Washington, the two men took advantage of an hour's free time to drive around the capital. Lo and behold, in the middle of Pennsylvania Avenue, there was a man urinating. Brezhnev pointed it out to Nixon. President Nixon immediately ordered the Secret Service to arrest the man and have him brought to the White House.

"You know, General Secretary Brezhnev," Nixon said glumly to the Kremlin boss, "that's the strangest thing. I've never before seen it happen in this city. I'm anxious to talk to the man. Ah, here he is now. You, sir, why were you peeing in the street?"

"Because that's the way it's done in my country," the man replied unabashedly.

"And who are you?" asked Nixon.

"I'm the Soviet ambassador to Washington!" replied the man.

An American and a Russian were arguing about whose country was the more democratic.

"Come on, Ivan, we have much more freedom in the United States. Look, I can go to Washington whenever I like, stand in front of the White House, and shout: 'The President is a big bum.' The President may not agree with me, but I can do it without getting arrested," boasted the American proudly.

"Big deal, Johnny. Anytime I want, I can go to Moscow, stand in front of the Kremlin and also shout: 'The American President is a big bum.' And not only will no one arrest me, but it's likely that our leader himself will come out to congratulate me!" retorted the Russian.

Seeking to leave the church quietly after the Easter service, Ivanov, the KGB agent, found himself facing his boss, Fyodorov, who was keeping an eye on religious believers.

"Ivanov, what were you doing in the church?" demanded Fyodorov. "I hope you're not a practicing Russian Orthodox."

"No, thank God, I'm an atheist," Ivanov blurted out.

Karl Marx was resurrected. Needless to say, he immediately went to the Soviet Union to have a look at the first country in the world to call itself a Marxist state. After touring a few cities and towns and several collective farms, he went to Moscow, where he requested the right to broadcast an hour-long speech on national television.

"We're terribly sorry, Comrade Marx," explained the director of broadcasting, "but we can't give you an hour. We're busy enough as it is broadcasting the many activities of our leader, the party's General Secretary."

"Well, how about, say, half an hour?" pleaded Marx.

"I'm afraid we can't even manage half an hour," the director apologized. "We have a forthcoming series on the leading role of the Communist party in the daily lives of our citizens, so we won't have any free time slots."

"That series sounds terribly important," responded Marx, "but couldn't you just find me a few seconds to address the Soviet people? That's surely the least you could do for me, the founder of Communism."

Unable to turn down such a request, the broadcasting director made the necessary arrangements to permit Marx to appear on national television for exactly five seconds. When the time came, Marx looked straight at the camera and said, "Workers of the world— I apologize."

"There's an exact double of you in Odessa," Secret Police Chief Beria informed Stalin. "In fact, he looks so identical, Josif Vissarionovich,[2] that it's impossible to tell you apart."

"Shoot him immediately," ordered Stalin.

"But maybe we could just shave his moustache?" suggested Beria.

"I suppose we could solve the problem that way, too," said Stalin.

A Soviet tourist in London approached a man at Piccadilly Circus.

"Excuse, please, me," said the Soviet in his best English. "Vat time have you?"

"I tree o'clock have," said the man, glancing at his watch.

"Ah," said the Soviet gleefully, switching to Russian, "you must also be a graduate of the Moscow Institute of Foreign Languages."

Brezhnev's deceased mother returned to earth to see how her son, Leonid, was doing. Anxious to make a good impression, he took her to see his well-appointed apartment, his spacious office in the Kremlin,

---

[2]Stalin's first name and patronymic.

and the several country homes at his personal disposal. He also
showed her the cars, yachts, jets, and helicopters that were for his use
only.

"Well, Mama, what do you think of all this?" he asked her.

"Son, I think it's absolutely wonderful that you've done so well,"
said his mother proudly, "but I've got one piece of advice for you. If I
were you, I'd grab the transportable goods, sell the rest, and run before
the Communists come to power and confiscate it all."

Stalin was addressing a party conference.

"Comrades, I repeat that there is nothing more important in the
Soviet Union than the value of a human life. Furthermore. . . ."

A sneeze in the hall interrupted Stalin's speech.

"Who sneezed?" demanded Stalin.

Silence.

"Beria," said the Soviet dictator, turning to the head of the secret
police, "shoot everyone in the first row."

Beria commanded his men to follow Stalin's order.

"Now, who sneezed?" demanded Stalin.

Again silence.

"Beria, order your men to kill everyone in the second row," the
dictator ordered.

The order was carried out.

"I want to know who sneezed," insisted Stalin.

No reply.

"Beria, take care of the third row," Stalin shouted.

All those in the third row were mowed down.

"I will ask one more time. Who sneezed?" Stalin screamed with
rage.

"I did, Comrade Stalin," came a quivering voice from the back of
the room.

"Good. I told all of you that there's nothing more important in this country than the value of human life. You, comrade, the one who sneezed, I want you to go home immediately, take two aspirins, and get plenty of rest," said Stalin, as he walked away from the podium.

How happy Brezhnev was to be at his *dacha* in the Crimea! The first morning he awoke early and went out onto the balcony to greet the sun.

"Good morning, beautiful sun," exclaimed the Soviet leader.

"Good morning, illustrious first secretary of our beloved party," the sun said brightly.

After a few hours of work in his office, Brezhnev again went outside, this time to see the warm, glowing afternoon sun overhead.

"Good afternoon, dear sun," shouted Brezhnev.

"Good afternoon, courageous hero of the anti-fascist war and beloved first citizen of our glorious homeland," the sun answered.

Brezhnev went back into the house, took a nap, and then did a few more hours of work before stepping out onto the balcony for a look at the sunset.

"Good evening, setting sun," said Brezhnev with a wave of the hand.

"Go to hell, you bastard," replied the sun. "I've made it to the West."

A news broadcast in the year 2025: All's quiet on the Chinese-Finnish border.

A delegation of American Communists arrived in Moscow. Soviet party official Petrov began explaining to the group how to propagandize among American workers toward the ultimate goal of the destruction of the capitalist system through a coalition of workers and other exploited members of American society.

"Remember, the most important thing is to convince the American working class that everything will be far better for them under Communism," emphasized Petrov.

When the meeting was over, Petrov approached the head of the American delegation. "So, my American comrade, is everything now clear?" he asked.

"Yes, comrade, with the exception of only one thing," said the American. "We still don't know how to explain to the American working class who would pay them unemployment benefits under Communism."

*Question:*  What's meant by an exchange of opinions in the Communist party of the Soviet Union?

*Answer:*   It's when I come to a party meeting with my own opinion, and I leave with the party's.

A group of American Communists arrived in Moscow to report on their activities in the United States.

"And how is the propaganda campaign doing?" the Central Committee official asked the American leader.

"Not well at all, comrade," admitted the America. "The problem is that American workers are always busy. If they're not redoing their homes, they're going on holidays in their recreation vehicles. If they're not watching their color television sets, they're out eating in Italian or Chinese restaurants. If they're not shopping or playing sports, they're visiting their children in college or at summer camp. The point is that they just don't have enough free time for us to explain how badly off they are under the capitalists."

In Tbilisi, the capital of Soviet Georgia, a free-wheeling Georgian was describing to a Russian his recent trip to Moscow.

"First, I went to the best hotel in Moscow and asked for a room. The manager said they were full up, so I pulled out a fifty-ruble note and slipped it to him. He gave me the best suite in the house.

"Then I went to the top restaurant in the city, and the *maître d'hôtel* told me that all the tables were reserved. So what did I do? I slipped him seventy-five rubles, and he gave me a beautiful table.

"Then I figured that as long as I was in Moscow, I should go to the Mausoleum in Red Square to see our beloved Lenin's resting place. So I walked up to the guard, ignoring the thousands of people waiting in line to get in, and slipped him 100 rubles. He got so excited he asked if I preferred to go right in to see Lenin's body or if I would rather have him bring the body out into the sunlight."

Napoleon and his aide-de-camp returned to earth and were invited by the Soviet leaders to attend the large military parade held in Moscow on November 7, the anniversary of the Bolshevik Revolution.

"Napoleon, Napoleon," exclaimed the aide-de-camp as the parade began, "just look at those guns. Oh, if only we had had such guns, can you imagine what we could have accomplished."

Napoleon, however, did not look at the guns, for he was busy reading a copy of *Pravda*, the Soviet newspaper.

"Napoleon, just look at that artillery," said the aide-de-camp a few minutes later. "Ah, the outcome of Waterloo would have been different if we had had such artillery."

Napoleon continued to read the newspaper.

"Napoleon," shouted the aide-de-camp, "look at those tanks. With such tanks, we could have rolled right over the enemy."

Napoleon's attention was still directed at the newspaper. A couple of minutes later, he lifted his head and said, "What's all this talk about guns, artillery, and tanks to defeat the enemy at Waterloo. Much too expensive and cumbersome. Ah, if only we had had newspapers like this *Pravda* here, then no one would ever have known that we lost at Waterloo!"

An American and a Russian were debating the question of whose country had the better intelligence service.

"The KGB is the best in the word," boasted the Russian. "I heard that they've managed to steal all the designs of the major American weapons systems for the last ten years."

"That's nothing, Ivan," the American retorted. "I know for a fact that the CIA has succeeded in stealing from the Kremlin's safe the results of all the Soviet elections for the next ten years!"

A delegation of American businessmen was touring the Soviet Union. The group was most impressed by the absence of strikes and labor difficulties in the country, problems they would have liked to do without in the United States. Their host, a senior party official, was so anxious to reinforce this difference between Soviet and American labor that he invited the delegation to attend a factory workers' meeting.

"Comrade workers," announced the party official to the assembled throng, "the party has decreed that beginning immediately all of you are to work sixteen hours per day, seven days a week, at no extra pay. Any questions?"

Absolute silence. The American businessmen couldn't believe their eyes and ears. If only it could be the same in America. . . .

"That's nothing," said the party official to the Americans. "Watch this. Comrade workers, your attention, please. The party has just decreed that the work day must be extended to twenty-four hours per day, seven days a week, no holidays, and no extra pay. Any questions?"

Again, silence. Again, amazement on the part of the Americans.

"That's still nothing," said the party official to the Americans. "Listen to this. Comrade workers, I must again revise what I've said. It's now in the interests of the party that all of you should be hanged tomorrow at dawn. Are there any questions?"

"Just one," came a voice from the crowd. "Are you providing the rope or shall we bring our own?"

*Question:* Why did *Pravda* adopt the following new format:

*Answer:* So that people would find it more difficult to read between the lines.

An archaeological mission went from Moscow to an area alongside the Turkish frontier to excavate a potentially important historical site. Because of the site's sensitive location, a KGB agent was assigned to the group.

After a few days of digging, the team came across a human skeleton, but the archaeologists were unable to determine just how old it might be. At this point, the KGB man asked whether he could be alone with the skeleton for a few minutes.

"The skeleton is exactly 1,568 years old," proudly announced the agent after only a couple of minutes.

"That's incredible!" exclaimed the archaeologists. "How did you figure it out?"

"Easy. I forced a confession out of him," said the agent.

UNESCO, in sponsoring an international symposium on elephants, asked a number of member countries to prepare papers for presentation.

The French submitted a study on "101 Ways to Make Love to an Elephant."

The Italians wrote on "Can an Elephant Be Trained as a Contralto?"

The Danes' study was on "1,001 Ways to Use Elephants in the Making of Open-faced Sandwiches."

The Germans' study focused on "The Racial Origin and Purity of Elephants."

The Jews' study looked at "Elephants and the Jewish Question."

And the Russian entry was entitled, "Soviet Elephants: The Greatest Elephants in the World."

*Question from Armenian Radio:* Is it really the interest of the Soviet people to send the first man to Mars?

*Answer:* Absolutely. Don't you realize that the first man in our country is our Soviet leader?

To celebrate the 125th anniversary of the birth of the famous Russian writer Nikolai Gogol, Stalin announced a nationwide art competition. Second prize went to the artist who painted a picture of Stalin reading one of Gogol's works. First prize went for a picture of Gogol reading one of Stalin's works!

The Czech authorities decided to open a naval ministry, but, as in all military matters, they first had to get Kremlin approval.

"Why would you have a naval ministry if you have no sea?" came the Soviet reply.

Forgetting for just a moment the nature of the bilateral relationship, the Czechs began to answer, "And why would you have a ministry of culture if you have no . . ."

*Question:* Was Comrade Gorbachev born on his birthday?

*Answer:* Yes, indeed. Ever since childhood our great leader has always loved precision.

In the 1940s, after the Baltic states were seized by the Soviet Union, a curious situation developed.

*Question:* Why is Lithuania the largest country in the world?

*Answer:*    Because it borders on the Baltic Sea, has its decisions made for it in Moscow, and counts the majority of its population in Siberia.

In the USSR, an innocent remark can get you into hot water.
    "What did they arrest Ivanov for?" his neighbor Petrov asked.
    "For asking a provocative question," replied Ivanov's wife.
    "What was the question?" asked Petrov.
    "He asked a shop clerk which tea was better—Chinese or Soviet," sighed the wife.

The Chinese high military command gathered in 1963 to hear the report of its chief of staff on a new battle plan to conquer the Soviet Union.
    "Officers, when the time for war comes, we'll position 100 million soldiers on the left flank and 100 million soldiers on the right flank and pour in our tanks down the middle," the military commander announced.
    "Excuse me, commander," interjected one officer, "but do you really mean to say that we're going to use both of our tanks right away?"

Just after the split in the early 1960s between Moscow and Peking, a Soviet official visiting Peking was asked to give his views on the reasons for the rift. He spoke in Russian to a large gathering for some ten minutes before pausing to give the interpreter time to translate. However, the interpreter said but one word in Chinese: "Dang." The crowd applauded enthusiastically.

Somewhat puzzled by the brief translation, but obviously encouraged by the reaction of the audience, the Soviet speaker went on with his speech. When he paused after another ten minutes to allow for translation, he was surprised to hear the interpreter say only: "Dong." This time the applause was still more thunderous.

When the visitor concluded the third and final part of his talk, the interpreter simply said to the audience: "Dung." The audience rose to its feet. There was unrestrained applauding, shouting, even foot-stomping.

The Soviet was so pleased by this response that he rushed up to the interpreter, gave him a big bear hug, and asked him how he had managed to compress so many words into so few.

"Simple," explained the Chinese interpreter. "After you finished the first part of your talk, I simply said 'Rubbish.' After the second part, I said, 'More rubbish.' And at the conclusion of your talk, all I said was 'End of rubbish.' "

A story of sophisticated technology.

"Ivan, did you hear that the Chinese launched a sputnik?" his friend asked.

"No kidding! I didn't think they had the technology to do that," said Ivan.

"Technology? What technology? They just got a couple of million people to pull the slingshot," laughed the friend.

*Question from Armenian Radio:* Is it possible to build Communism in, say, Holland?

*Answer:*    Yes, but what do you have against Holland?

An old Bolshevik, one of Lenin's closest compatriots, was dying. To honor him, the government asked what his last wish was.

"I would like to see everything in the GUM[3] department store given away rather than sold for three days," said the old man, his voice choked with emotion.

"Old comrade," announced a government official, "your wish shall be granted."

A sign was posted at the entrance to the store announcing that for the next three days all merchandise would be given away free. The first day, the crowds were so heavy that the police had to be called. By the second day, word of the event had spread throughout Moscow, and hundreds of thousands of people turned out. The crowds were so thick, the crush so great, the pushing and shoving so intense, the arguments and fights so numerous that the army had to be brought in. Full riot gear, water hoses, tear gas, and numerous arrests were needed to restore some semblance of order. The government official who had originally authorized the giveaway rushed to the bedside of the old Bolshevik.

"Tell me, old comrade, why did you have this idea to give everything away?" he complained. "We've had nothing but bedlam, rioting, and even bloodshed."

"Forgive me, comrade, but I only wanted to see how everything would be when we finally reached the last stage of Communism."

---

[3]Moscow's main department store.

*Question:*  What is the difference between the American Mafia and the
Soviet Mafia?

*Answer:*  The American Mafia works against the government, but
the Soviet Mafia *is* the government.

An American agricultural delegation visited a Soviet collective farm.
Out in the fields they noticed two men at work. The first would take
his shovel and dig a hole. The second would come up behind him and
fill the hole. The pattern repeated itself for an hour or more.

"I don't understand what those two men are doing," commented
one of the Americans to the farm manager.

"Well, you see normally they work in teams of three. The first digs
the hole, the second plants the sapling, and the third fills the hole. The
second man is sick today, but we didn't want to waste the time of the
other two!" the manager explained.

Ivan dutifully went to the polling booth on election day. He was
handed an envelope containing the name of the candidate for whom
the party had directed him to vote. Ivan immediately began to open it.

"What are you doing?" shouted the party official.

"I only wanted to see the name of the person I'm to vote for,"
meekly replied Ivan.

"What's the matter with you?" asked the official. "Don't you
realize the voting is secret? Open the envelope when you get *behind* the
curtain."

After the first day's round of talks at the White House, Nixon accompanied Brezhnev to the guest room.

"Mr. General Secretary," said Nixon, "I hope you'll have a good night's rest."

"Thank you, Mr. President," replied Brezhnev.

The next morning, they met for breakfast.

"And so, Mr. General Secretary, how did you sleep?" asked Nixon.

"Quite well, thank you, but I had a dream that kept appearing all during the night," Brezhnev said.

"About what?" asked Nixon.

"I dreamed that I returned to Washington ten years from now, and when I disembarked at the airport, I saw red flags flying over all the buildings. Then I drove into Washington, and the entire route was lined with red flags. Finally, I arrived at the White House where there was also a red flag flying high," said Brezhnev.

"But that's terrible, Mr. General Secretary," moaned Nixon. "That means we will have lost our precious American way of life."

A few months later, Nixon paid a state visit to the Soviet Union. After the first day's meetings, Brezhnev wished Nixon a good night's rest, and they agreed to meet again in the morning.

"So, Mr. President, how did you enjoy sleeping in a good Soviet bed?" inquired Brezhnev the next day.

"Just fine, thank you, but every few minutes the same dream would come to me," replied Nixon.

"How interesting!" commented Brezhnev. "And what sort of a dream was it?"

"Well, you see, I dreamed that I returned to Moscow a few years from now, and everywhere I looked there were red flags—red flags at the airport, lining the highways, on all the major buildings," said Nixon.

"You can't imagine, Mr. President, how happy you make me," Brezhnev began. "That only underscores the strength of our Communist system and . . ."

"But there was something funny about the flags," interjected Nixon. "They had writing on them."

"What did they say?" asked Brezhnev, a puzzled expression on his face.

"I don't know," confessed Nixon, "I can't read Chinese."

A headline in a Kiev newspaper shortly after the Chernobyl accident: "Even Soviet Disasters Are the Greatest in the World."

*Question:* What is the difference between Catholicism and Communism?

*Answer:* In Catholicism there is life after death. In Communism there is posthumous rehabilitation.

In Vilnius, the capital of Lithuania, a stronghold of Catholicism, the party chief was troubled by the church's continuing success in attracting adherents. He decided to meet with the archbishop to learn something about the church's techniques.

"Help me to understand," the party boss began, "why you people draw so many new members when we can't get anyone to join."

"It's really very simple," the cleric responded. "Your promised paradise is right here for everyone to see and judge. Ours is not."

*Question:* What's the definition of a Soviet string quartet?

*Answer:*    A Soviet symphony orchestra that just returned from a
tour of the West.

In the propaganda war against the United States, the Odessa party
chief had an idea. He placed an order with an American manufacturer
for ten million condoms of what he called standard Soviet medium
size: fifteen inches long and five inches wide.

*Question:* Why do Soviet policemen always travel in groups of three?

*Answer:*    Because one knows how to read, the second knows how to
write, and the third is in charge of controlling these two
dangerous intellectuals!

At an Odessa police station, the officer-in-charge instructed his men
to check the documents of everyone on the street that day.

Following these orders, Officers Ivanov, Komarenko, and Fyodorov diligently scrutinized the internal passports and residence per-
mits of those they came across in their assigned district. But when a
penguin approached, they weren't sure what to do.

"An order is an order," insisted Ivanov. "We'll have to take him in
if he doesn't have the proper papers."

And so the three policemen arrested the penguin and brought him to the precinct house. When the officer-in-charge saw them, he demanded an explanation.

"But you told us to bring in anyone whose documents weren't in order. This penguin didn't have a single piece of identification," the officers protested.

"Get that penguin out of here," commanded the officer-in-charge. "Take him to the zoo."

The next day, the officer-in-charge was driving around the precinct in his patrol car when he noticed the same three policemen standing on a ticket line at a movie theater. And who was with them? The penguin. And the four were talking it up and laughing. Infuriated, he ran up to them.

"What's going on here?" he shouted. "Didn't I tell you yesterday to take this penguin to the zoo?"

"That's exactly what we did," replied Ivanov. "Yesterday we took him to the zoo, and today we thought we'd take him to the movies."

At the opening of the 1980 Summer Olympic Games in Moscow, Brezhnev was the featured speaker. Amidst great fanfare, he approached the microphone, took out the prepared remarks from his pocket, and started to read aloud.

"O, O, O. . . ," the Soviet leader began.

An aide quickly rushed to Brezhnev's side and whispered in his ear, "Leonid Ilich, you're not reading the right text. That's the Olympic symbol."

In view of the very low birth rate in the European part of the USSR, the Odessa City Committee of the Communist party instructed the local biological research institute to find an effective means of artificial insemination. Within a short time, the institute's director reported that research findings were encouraging; a woman had been found to test the new procedure and the results would be reported on in nine months.

The party leader was dissatisfied with the news. Being impatient for progress, he sent a directive to the institute's director ordering him to locate three women instead and report the findings in three months.

Soviet readers are confronted with a sad reality about the country's two leading newspapers: There is no *pravda*[4] in *Izvestiya* and no *izvestiya*[5] in *Pravda*.

A German, a Japanese, a Jew, and a Russian all met God in heaven.

"And what can I do for you?" God asked the German.

"I wish that Germany were once again united," he replied.

"Your wish shall be granted," said God. "And who is next?"

"I always want the sun to rise over Japan," requested the Japanese.

"Your wish, too, shall be granted. And," turning to the Jew, "what about you?" God asked.

"It's my greatest hope that Israel will survive and one day live in peace," the Jew responded.

"Yes, indeed," God replied. "And what does the fourth person desire?"

---

[4]Truth (Russian).

[5]News (Russian).

"Only this," began the Russian. "Please assure me that the next time I stand in line, they'll still have whatever they are selling by the time I reach the counter."

Khrushchev, being particularly interested in agriculture, visited a collective farm.

"What did you do this morning?" the Soviet leader asked one of the workers.

"We planted potatoes," came the response.

"Excellent. And what did you do in the afternoon?" Khrushchev continued.

"We dug them out," the worker replied, speaking for the group.

"But why?" asked the Soviet leader.

"Because we were hungry," they said in unison.

During Khrushchev's state visit to the United States, he was especially interested in learning about the American farming techniques that had produced such successful harvests year after year, whereas the Soviet Union endured chronic food shortages. Immediately upon his return to the USSR, he went to visit an agricultural settlement where he was struck by the fact that the farmers were eating the hay.

"What's the matter with you?" Khrushchev exclaimed. "Learn from the Americans. I just returned from a visit there where I had the chance to consult with some of their leading agronomists. Their advice to our farmers was to eat the grass now and save the hay for winter meals."

In a relaxed moment, Gorbachev agreed to an informal meeting with a few journalists.

"Who do you think will govern South Africa in the year 2000?" Gorbachev was asked in the off-the-record interview.

"White people," he responded immediately.

"And how much is a pound of butter in South Africa likely to cost?" he was asked.

"Fifty rubles," he speculated.

Sign at the entrance to an Odessa bakery during one of the country's periodic food shortages: "Man Does Not Live by Bread Alone."

When Stalin died in 1953, St. Peter sent him directly to hell. The next day, some devils appeared before St. Peter.

"What do you want?" the keeper of the gates inquired.

"Asylum. We're refugees from hell," they replied.

A resident of East Germany went to consult with a doctor.

"Doctor, you must help me," pleaded the man. "I suffer from a recurring nightmare."

"Describe it to me," said the doctor.

"I want to defect. Every night I have this same horrendous vision," groaned the patient.

"To be perfectly honest, it's really quite a normal thought in our country. Practically everyone wants to cross the border," the doctor said in a soothing tone.

"But the problem is that in my nightmares I want to defect to Poland, not West Germany," cried the man.

In the year 2001, a man was walking with his grandson near Chernobyl. They passed an enormous pit.

"Do you know what used to be here?" the grandfather asked.

"Yes, part of the atomic reactor," the child replied.

"Good boy," the grandfather said, as he patted his grandson on the head.

They continued walking until they approached another pit. "And what used to stand here?" he asked the boy.

"Another part of the reactor," said the boy.

"Clever fellow," the grandfather said, as he patted his grandson on his other head.

*Question from Armenian Radio:* What is the definition of an unbending Communist?

*Answer:*   A Communist with arthritis.

Two Soviet planes were flying from Moscow to Kabul, Afghanistan's capital. One was loaded with ammunition, the other with food. The first landed safely in Kabul; the second was shot down near Moscow.

An American tourist visiting the Soviet Union in the 1920s approached a man on a Moscow street.

"What's the difference in political structure between the United States and the Soviet Union?" he asked.

"Just like in your country, we also have two political parties," the Soviet replied. "The only difference is that while one is in power, the other is in jail."

An American industrial delegation visited the Soviet Union.

"We Soviets produce 10,000 cars per year," the Soviet minister of heavy industry boasted.

"Big deal," replied one of the Americans. "We Americans steal 10,000 cars per year."

Two skeletons met at an Odessa cemetery.

"Did you die before Gorbachev started his campaign to increase the food supply?" asked the first.

"Yes. How about you?" asked the other.

"No, I'm still alive," replied the first.

After Khrushchev's denunciation of Stalin, the Soviet leader ordered the removal of the tyrant's body from the Mausoleum in Moscow's Red Square.

"But Comrade Stalin, why are you moving from here?" asked his embalmed neighbor Lenin.

"I'm bored living in this communal apartment of ours," complained Stalin. "They say the housing shortage in our country is now over, and I was told I could get a place of my own."

Mr. and Mrs. Smirnoff emigrated to the United States. At New York's Kennedy Airport, they noticed their first ad in capitalist America.

"Tell me what it says, dear," the husband asked.

"America loves Smirnoff," she read.

"Didn't I tell you this was going to be a wonderful country!" he exclaimed.

Foreign Minister Gromyko was on the telephone from the Kremlin with Secretary of State Kissinger.

"No," shouted the veteran Soviet diplomat into the receiver. "No, no, no, yes."

Brezhnev, who was sitting nearby, became angry.

"Why did you say 'yes?' I told you never to say 'yes' to the Americans," Brezhnev shouted.

"Because his fifth question to me was: 'Mr. Gromyko, can you hear me?'" came the reply.

When Eduard Shevardnadze, the Soviet foreign minister, returned from his first trip abroad, he recounted the experience to his wife.

"I have to confess that, due to my newness at the job and the pressures on me, I made some mistakes in dates," he sighed wearily. "For example, when I met the pope, I said: 'Your Holiness, please accept my heartfelt condolences in connection with the attempt on your life.' The surprised pope looked at me and replied: 'But that was years ago.'

"Then we went to London where I met Margaret Thatcher. The first thing I said to her was: 'Madam Prime Minister, I was so sorry to hear about the attempt on your life.' She said that she knew absolutely nothing about any such incident. That evening I returned to my hotel room and checked my notebook. You know, she was absolutely right," admitted the diplomat. "The assassination plot against her was planned for next month."

*Question:* What's the difference between capitalist and Communist grammar?

*Answer:* In capitalist grammar there are three verb tenses—past, present, and future; but in Communist grammar there is only one—future—as in "there will be meat," "we will be happy," "we will surpass the Americans," and "we will prevail."

An ad in a Chernobyl newspaper in 1987: "A Radioactive Man Seeks Radiopassive Wife."

When you're hot, you're hot!

"Today's weather in Chernobyl," the television announcer began, "is expected to be sunny with only a slight chance of rain. The maximum temperature is likely to reach 1,580 degrees Fahrenheit."

*Question:* Why are advancements in laser technology so important to the Soviet food industry?

*Answer:* So that scarce meat can be sliced even thinner.

*Question:* What is the ratio between a dollar, a pound, and a ruble?

*Answer:* In Odessa for a pound of rubles you can get a dollar.

An American tourist walking in Red Square noticed a person near the Kremlin wall carrying a flag.

"What's the holiday?" the American asked a passer-by.

"No holiday," the Soviet replied. "That's a famous journalist of ours. Every day on his way to work he stands with that flag in front of the Kremlin to find out which way the wind is blowing."

As the victorious Red Army entered Romania at the end of World War II, a Soviet soldier noticed a local farmer standing near his barn.

"Excuse me, what time is it?" the young Soviet asked.

"In ten minutes I'll let you know," came the reply.

The farmer took a long stick and drove it into the ground. He then carefully measured the sun's shadow. "I would say it's half past two," the farmer finally declared.

The soldier pulled up the sleeve of his army jacket to reveal a dozen purloined watches on his left arm. He glanced at them. "That's correct," he said. "Now hand over the stick."

Under Gorbachev's reign, a measure of private enterprise was introduced; some small shops were opened. A young woman entered one such shop in search of pacifiers for her baby.

"I need some pacifiers badly," she announced to the shop's owner. "Give me six."

"That will be a ruble each," said the shopkeeper.

"What!" protested the customer. "In the drugstore, they only cost ten kopecks a piece."

"So why don't you go buy them there?" asked the shopkeeper.

"Because they're sold out," said the annoyed woman.

"Listen, lady, if I were sold out of pacifiers, I could also afford to sell them for ten kopecks apiece," replied the shopkeeper with a grin.

Communism is the most equitable system in the world. After all, in other countries either the government steals from the people or the people steal from the government. Under Communism, however, the government steals as much as possible from the people while the people are stealing all they can from the government.

*Question on Armenian Radio:* Is it true that the tap dance was invented
in America?

*Answer:*   False. It was invented in the USSR.

*Question:* But how can you be certain?

*Answer:*   It was invented by the residents of a Soviet communal
apartment. You'd be tap dancing too if you shared a flat
with fifteen other people and had only one toilet among
you.

At a congress in Moscow, a Soviet scientist and an American scientist
decided to go outside, where the Soviet felt a little more comfortable
chatting. As they walked toward the exit, the Soviet lugged along two
heavy suitcases, which the American discreetly chose to ignore.

"Tell me, my Soviet friend, what do you do when you want to
measure the time of something? What sort of stopwatch do you use?"
asked the American.

"Well," replied the Soviet, "I simply push these buttons on my
watch here and, within a few seconds, I have the answer."

"And what do you do if you want to recall a number?" the
American continued.

"Well, I simply push these other buttons here and retrieve it from
the watch's memory," the Soviet explained.

"That's good. Tell me, what sort of watch is it? Japanese?" asked
the curious American.

"No. It's Soviet," said the Russian.

"Amazing. I didn't realize that you Soviets built such watches.
Your country ought to be exporting them, competing with Seiko and
others," said the American.

"We would if we could only solve one problem," admitted the Soviet scientist.

"What's that?" the American scientist replied.

"What to do about these two batteries," said the Soviet, pointing to the two suitcases. "Carrying them around is killing my arms."

During the period of Stalin's Great Terror in the 1930s, this scenario was frequently heard.

"How long are you here for?" the prison guard asked the newly arrived inmate.

"Ten years," the prisoner replied.

"What did you do?" asked the guard.

"Nothing," came the reply.

"That's not possible," said the guard. "For nothing, they give you five years, not ten."

Brezhnev rushed into the Politburo meeting ten minutes late, took out a piece of paper from his coat, and began to read aloud his long-anticipated report.

"My dear comrades, the unexpected death of the General Secretary of our Communist party, our beloved Leonid Ilich Brezhnev, is a tragic loss for the party and the people. . . . Oops, wait a second," said Brezhnev as he checked the coat he was wearing, "I think I've taken the wrong coat. Does anyone recognize this one?"

"Yes, it's mine," said an embarrassed Yuri Andropov, head of the KGB.

When President Nixon arrived in Moscow, a Soviet journalist approached him.

"Mr. President, during your stay here would you like to see a striptease show?" asked the newsman.

"Is it possible to see a striptease show in Moscow?" the surprised president asked.

"No, actually it isn't. In fact, it is specifically forbidden," replied the journalist.

"Frankly, it doesn't matter," said Nixon. "I'm not really interested in that sort of entertainment."

The next day the lead paragraph of the journalist's story read as follows: "Richard Nixon, president of the United States, arrived in our capital yesterday. His first question to this reporter was: 'Is it possible to see a striptease show in Moscow?'"

An ad appeared in a Kiev[6] newspaper shortly after the 1986 disaster at the Chernobyl nuclear power plant: "Prepared to exchange a lovely apartment in Kiev for equivalent place anywhere in the world except Hiroshima, Nagasaki, or Three Mile Island."

Each time the Moscow-based foreign press corps saw Gorbachev's chauffeur, Petya, they would try to pump him for information about the war in Afghanistan.

"Come on, tell us," they would say, "maybe you've overheard a conversation suggesting when the war in Afghanistan would end."

---

[6]Kiev is the largest city in the proximity of Chernobyl.

"No, I simply don't know. Gorbachev has said nothing about that," was the standard reply.

One day, though, a reporter had some better luck. "Is it really possible that Gorbachev never says anything at all about the war?" he asked the chauffeur.

"No, as a matter of fact just this morning he raised the issue with me," Petya admitted.

"Well, what did he say?" demanded the reporter.

"As we were driving from his house to the Kremlin," the chauffeur began, "he turned to me and said: 'Petya, do you have any idea when this damned war in Afghanistan is going to end?'"

During elections in Leningrad, some voters complained to party officials that they didn't know the names of the candidates.

"Remember, comrades, the balloting in our country is secret," explained a local official.

"That's all well and good," responded a spokesman for the disgruntled voters, "but in this era of *glasnost* we feel we have a right to know names."

"I suppose you have a point," conceded the official. "First, go and vote. Then we'll tell you the names of the winners."

To streamline production at "The Red October" factory in Odessa, and as part of Gorbachev's campaign to modernize the Soviet economy, new equipment was purchased from Sweden that could carry out the work of 100 employees. Since its installation, the machinery has aroused enormous curiosity. All day long, day after day, the 100 salaried employees stand around and watch the equipment at work.

In a Soviet classroom, a history lesson was in progress.

"Class, who can tell me the name of the first man? Yes, Anna," said the teacher, turning to a girl in the first row.

"The first man was our beloved leader, Comrade Vladimir Ilich Lenin," the child replied confidently.

"No, Anna," explained the teacher. "I mean in the broader sense. The first man was, in fact, Adam."

"I suppose that's true, teacher," said the little girl, "if you start with the capitalists."

The problem of service continues to plague Soviet consumer life, as two American tourists discovered in the dining room of a Moscow hotel when they ordered coffee.

"Waiter, this is filthy," said one of the Americans on seeing the coffee placed before them. "Please bring clean cups."

A few minutes later, the waiter returned with two cups of coffee. "Now which one of you ordered the clean cup?" he asked.

At KGB headquarters in Moscow, a high-level meeting was underway.

"We've just learned that the Czechs are amassing their army near the border and planning to attack us," an intelligence official advised his superior.

"But what could possibly be their motivation?" the startled boss inquired.

"Well, you remember 1968 when we invaded Czechoslovakia because of Dubcek's effort to democratize their country," explained the official. "Now they say it's time to invade us because of Gorbachev's effort to democratize ours."

In another KGB office, ten years earlier, this exchange was taking place.

"What's your opinion about Brezhnev?" a KGB official asked his assistant.

"Why, the same as yours, of course," came the reply.

"In that case, I'm obliged to arrest you," the official said.

In the early 1950s, a still rare German tourist was visiting Prague, Communist Czechoslovakia's capital. Strolling in the evening in the city center, he was set upon by three men and robbed. Urged to act by passers-by, he reported the incident to the police.

"What happened?" the police inspector asked.

"Three Swiss soldiers robbed me and stole my Soviet-made gold watch," the German hesitantly explained, fearful of an adverse reaction to his German nationality with memories of the war still fresh.

"That's rather strange," said the puzzled inspector. "Are you sure you're not a bit confused? As far as I know, there are no Swiss soldiers in Czechoslovakia and never before have I heard of a Soviet gold watch. In my opinion, it must have been the reverse—the soldiers were Russian and the gold watch was Swiss."

"You said it, not me," said the German.

Two Soviet journalists were traveling together around the United States on assignment for their newspapers.

"Maybe it's true that in surgery the Americans are ahead of us, but they certainly lag far behind in public health," said one to the other smugly. "I haven't seen a single delousing station since we arrived in this country."

The Soviet Ministry of Public Health issued a new decree whereby those patients diagnosed to have serious illnesses were entitled to a second opinion before surgery.

"You are extremely ill," the doctor explained to Ivan. "I would say you have gangrene. That will require amputation of the lower part of your leg. And if you want a second opinion, I would say that if it's not gangrene, then it must be arthritis, in which case a daily dose of aspirin should be sufficient."

Three American spies parachuted into the Soviet Union, but one was captured shortly after landing. After spending several years in a Soviet prison, he was exchanged for a Soviet spy held in America. As soon as the American arrived in Washington, he was taken to his agency's headquarters for a debriefing.

"Tell us, Smith, how come you were caught so quickly?" the officer assigned to the case asked.

"Actually, it was because I hadn't been properly briefed. As it turned out, according to an old and still very popular Russian tradition, three men meet, buy a bottle of vodka between them, and drink it straightaway.

"Having landed near a small town, I hid my parachute and cautiously approached what seemed to be the main street. Remember, I was unaware of that Russian drinking custom.

"Noticing an open shop, I entered. It turned out that it was a kind of liquor store. These two men were standing near the cashier, and when they saw me, one joyously said, 'Finally, here is the third.' I assumed that Jones and Brown had already been arrested, so I raised my hands and confessed that I, too, was a spy!" explained Smith.

Two friends were sitting on a streetcar exchanging riddles.

"What's the difference between a napkin and our leaders?" Anatoly asked.

"I don't know," Leonid replied.

"A napkin is used to wipe your mouth; our leaders should only be used to wipe another part of your body," Anatoly laughed in reply.

A burly man wearing dark glasses overheard the exchange. "I see that the two of you like riddles," he said. "Well I've got one for you. What's the difference between the driver of this streetcar and the two of you?"

Neither friend ventured an answer.

"Let me tell you," the man said, a threatening tone in his voice. "The driver will remain in that seat of his up front to the very end of this ride; but the two of you will get off and follow me to police headquarters at the next stop."

When Brezhnev visited Czechoslovakia, the traditional twenty-one gun salute awaited him at the airport ceremony. Each shot could be heard across Prague.

After the second salvo, an elderly lady turned to her friend at an outdoor cafe and asked, "Why have they fired twice?"

"Brezhnev arrived," the friend replied.

"And what, our incompetent soldiers couldn't kill him with the first shot?" the old lady sneered.

In the USSR, political indoctrination begins early.

Little Ivan proudly announced to his teacher, "Our cat just gave birth. As my father said, now we have six new little Communists."

The teacher was very pleased. "Your father put it very well," she said. "Please send him my best regards."

A week passed. "So how are your six little Communists?" the teacher asked Ivan.

"As my father said, only five of them remain," said Ivan.

"Oh what a shame," sympathized the teacher. "Did the sixth Communist die?"

"No, he opened his eyes," the boy replied.

An American trade union delegation visited a Soviet factory. Anxious to meet a typical employee, they approached Ivanov, an assembly-line worker.

"Tell us, please, what's your attitude to your job in a country they call the workers' paradise?" one of the visitors asked.

"It's very simple. They pretend to pay us, and we pretend to work," came the reply.

A travel poster was displayed in the Intourist[7] office in Kabul, Afghanistan's capital, in December 1978, one year before the Soviet invasion. The text read: "Visit the USSR or else it will visit you!"

"My apartment is cramped and my pension is inadequate," Lenin's widow complained to Stalin.

"If you continue to complain," Stalin responded, "I'll be forced to appoint a new widow for our beloved Comrade Lenin."

An American tourist entered a Moscow butcher shop.

"I'm giving a party tonight for some friends," he said to the clerk. "Please wrap up ten steaks."

"I'll be happy to," smiled the clerk. "Give me the steaks."

To impress overseas tourists, a sign appeared at the entrance to a Moscow restaurant frequented by foreigners: "If we are not able to serve your favorite food, we'll pay you 100 rubles."

A group of Australian visitors decided to take up the challenge. To their amazement, however, the kitchen seemed to be coming up with every single outlandish order they placed, or so it appeared until the head waiter approached Fraser.

---

[7]The official Soviet travel agency.

"I am so sorry, sir," said the waiter, rather distressed. "We are not able to serve you the fried kangaroo tail with french fried potatoes that you ordered. Here are 100 rubles."

"I knew I could stump you with that order for kangaroo tail," boasted Fraser.

"Oh, that wasn't the problem at all," the waiter quickly explained. "In fact, one of our employees immediately went to the zoo and brought back a kangaroo. But we couldn't find any potatoes for the french fries."

While addressing an international conference of physicists, a member of the Soviet delegation referred to Ivanov–Newton's law of gravity.

"Why do you call it Ivanov–Newton's law of gravity?" protested a British participant. "Everyone knows that the law of gravity is associated entirely with the great seventeenth century English scientist, Sir Isaac Newton."

"Newton may have discovered the law," the Soviet countered, "but according to our leading scientist, Ivanov, gravity existed in Russia even before Newton discovered it."

Later, at the same physics conference, another Soviet boasted that x-rays were a Russian invention.

"Wrong," interjected an American delegate. "X-rays were discovered by the German physicist, Wilhelm Roentgen, in 1895. In fact, he even received the Nobel Prize a few years later for his great work. This time you Russians can't get away with such a ludicrous assertion."

"Not true," calmly responded the Soviet as he pulled out a tattered book. "Let me quote from this eighteenth-century work found in Odessa. It says:

The husband returned home early in the morning. His wife was waiting for him at the door. "Where have you been?" she demanded to know. "Uh, uh, I had to work very late," he sheepishly replied. "Nonsense," she said. "You've been out with another woman, haven't you? I can see right through you, you bastard."

"There you have the irrefutable proof that we Russians employed the principle of x-rays long before anyone else," the Soviet insisted.

A classified ad in an East German newspaper: "Prepared to exchange a luxury apartment in East Berlin for a hole in the Wall."

Two Russians met in a cafe in an isolated, economically depressed Siberian town.

"Ivan, I hate this God-forsaken place. By the way, I've got a terrific new joke to tell you about our leader," said Vasya.

"Shhh, Vasya," cautioned Ivan. "You know what happens to people who are overheard telling such jokes."

"But that's precisely the point," Vasya replied. "If people from Moscow are sent into internal exile in Siberia for three years for telling a good joke, then why shouldn't those of us from Siberia be sent into exile in Moscow for three years for the same offense."

Before the Bolshevik Revolution, Soviet Eskimos had two senses—a sense of hunger and a sense of cold. Since 1917 they haven't lost either sense, but have been compelled to add a third—a sense of gratitude to the Soviet Communist party for permitting them to continue to have the other two.

On the Romanian side of the Soviet-Romanian border, a lone guard suddenly noticed an armed Soviet convoy moving quickly in his direction. Fearful that this might be the long-expected Soviet invasion to crush the iconoclastic regime in Bucharest, the guard hurriedly alerted regional headquarters.

"It'll take us at least one hour to get reinforcements up there," said the commanding officer. "In the meantime, try to stop them."

"B-b-b-b-ut how?" stammered the Romanian guard.

"That's your business," replied the commanding officer.

An hour later, Romanian army officials arrived at the border area only to see the Soviet troops rushing back home.

"Absolutely amazing," said the admiring commanding officer to the sentry. "How did you do it?"

"Well, I simply stopped the lead truck, approached the Soviet driver, squinted, and said, 'Solly, long dilection.' You wouldn't believe how quickly he did a U-turn."

Question: What is the principal difference between capitalist and Communist agriculture?

Answer: In capitalist agriculture, the harvest is gathered every autumn. In Communist agriculture, the members of the Central Committee of the Communist party are gathered every autumn to be informed of the latest reason for another bad harvest.

More UNESCO research on elephants:

*From Bulgaria:*   "The Bulgarian Elephant: The Younger Brother of the Leading Soviet Elephant."

*From China:*   "The Elephant of Taiwan: A Member of the Great Family of Chinese Elephants."

*From East Germany:*   "The Importance of the Berlin Wall to the Survival and Reproduction of Elephants."

*From South Africa:*   "Keeping the Elephant in Its Proper Place."

*From the United States:*   "Breeding Ever Bigger Elephants."

*From the USSR:*   "Russia, the Motherland of All Elephants.

*Question:*   How could you tell when you were following the car of Yugoslav leader, Marshal Tito?

*Answer:*   Easy. He would always signal to the right but turn to the left.

Ayatollah Khomeini was becoming increasingly agitated with the prolonged war against Iraq. Anxious for a quick victory, he summoned his minister of defense.

"Do you remember the Russian one-eyed general who defeated Napoleon's forces?" the Iranian leader asked.

"Of course. It was Kutuzov," the minister promptly replied.

"And do you recall the one-eyed Jew who crushed Nasser?" the Ayatollah demanded to know.

"Sure. That was Moshe Dayan," the defense minister recalled.

"So what are you waiting for?" shouted Khomeini. "I want you to remove one eye immediately. Then we'll be able to rout the enemy."

*Question from Armenian Radio:* What do the United States and the Soviet Union have in common?

*Answer:*    The ruble isn't worth anything in either country.

*Question:* What is the Soviet Union's main goal in Afghanistan?

*Answer:*    To substitute the Soviet people for the Afghan people.

Ivan met his friend at a cafeteria.

"Why are you eating dinner here?" the surprised friend asked. "I heard that you got married not too long ago."

"True, but my wife doesn't know how to cook yet. In fact, she's attending a cooking class," the newlywed said proudly.

One year later, Ivan and his friend again ran into each other at the same cafeteria.

"What are you doing here? Didn't your wife learn anything in that class of hers?" the friend asked, rather shocked to see Ivan there again.

"As a matter of fact, she has, but nothing yet about cooking. They've finished studying the emergence of Marxist thought in the nineteenth century and are now about to discuss the Bolshevik Revolution," Ivan explained with a sigh.

Gorbachev ordered an end to the censorship of mail, but he warned that letters containing anti-Soviet comments would not be delivered.

The slogan at the practice range of the Soviet artillery regiment near Odessa: "Our Target Is Communism."

*Question on Armenian Radio:* What is the difference between the American and Soviet Constitutions?

*Answer:*   The Constitution of the Soviet Union guarantees freedom of assembly and freedom of speech. The Constitution of the United States guarantees freedom *after* assembly and *after* speech.

At Brezhnev's funeral, his octogenarian associates slowly carried the coffin to the Kremlin wall where he was buried.

The next day, on Armenian Radio, the following was heard:

*Question:* What is the difference between the deceased leader and his colleagues?

*Answer:*   Only their body temperature.

Two ardent Communist party officials in Kiev received a priority order to eradicate all vestiges of religion in the Ukrainian capital. They promptly went to the nearest church. An elderly woman was kneeling near the altar in silent prayer. They rushed up to her.

"What are you praying about?" they demanded to know.

"I am asking God to protect our leader, all the members of the Central Committee of the Communist party, and our other government officials," she responded.

"But, old woman, there is no God. I can prove it," said one official.

"How?" the old woman wanted to know.

"Well, admit that seventy-five years ago, just before our successful Bolshevik Revolution, you prayed for the health and well-being of your beloved Czar, didn't you?" he asked.

"And you remember what happened, don't you?" she replied with a twinkle in her eye.

*Question from Armenian Radio:* Who invented Communism? Scientists or politicians?

*Answer:*    Politicians, of course. Scientists would have first tested it out on animals.

A psychiatric examination of a village idiot.

"What is your name?" the doctor asked.

"Blah-blah-blah," was the only reply.

"Well, maybe you know how old you are," the doctor urged.

"Blah-blah-blah," was the only reply.

"What day is today?" asked the doctor, hoping for a response.

"Blah-blah-blah," was the only reply.

"What were your parents' names?" the doctor inquired, despairing of the answer.

"Blah-blah-blah," was the only reply.

"What is Communism?" the doctor asked, ready to admit that this patient was beyond help.

"The most progressive force in our society and the greatest hope for mankind," the idiot responded loudly.

*Question:* What is the necessary transitional stage between socialism and Communism?

*Answer:*    Alcoholism.

Two friends, standing in line, struck up a conversation.

"Ivanov, is the Communist Revolution still alive?" his friend Petrov asked.

"Yes," replied Ivanov, "and on display at the Central Museum of the Revolution, Monday through Friday, 10 A.M. to 4 P.M."

Ivanov was strolling near a river when he noticed a person drowning. Without a moment's hesitation, he plunged into the icy waters and managed a heroic rescue. It turned out the near victim was none other than Stalin himself.

"You are my savior," declared the Soviet dictator. "Your wish is my command. What shall it be?"

"I want to be buried in the Kremlin cemetery as soon as possible," replied Ivanov.

"But why? Are you fatally ill?" asked Stalin solicitously.

"No, as a matter of fact I'm quite healthy. But as soon as my friends hear that I've saved you from certain death, that's the only place I'll be safe from them," Ivanov explained.

Ivanov had finally saved enough money to purchase a car.[8] He went to the appropriate office and paid the money.

"Your car will be delivered exactly ten years from today," the clerk advised Ivanov.

"Morning or afternoon," Ivanov asked.

"Why is it so important for you to know that now?" the clerk asked, puzzled by the question.

"Because the plumber is coming that morning," was the immediate reply.

*Question:* What is the acronym for Gorbachev's policies of *glasnost, perestroyka,*[9] and *uskoreniye*[10]?

*Answer:*   GPU.[11]

---

[8]According to *The New York Times* (August 21, 1987), this is a favorite joke of President Reagan, one that he has used in a number of speeches.

[9]Reconstruction (Russian).

[10]Speeding up (Russian).

[11]The political or secret police that was established by Lenin in 1922 and abolished by Stalin in 1934, only to be replaced by the NKVD and later the KGB.

Brezhnev and Kosygin were meeting late one night.

"Why is our economy faltering?" Brezhnev asked Kosygin.

"Because we're not doing a good enough job of selecting the right people for the key jobs. I hear in the West that psychologists have created some very effective tests to screen applicants. Maybe we should begin using these tests here," Kosygin suggested.

"What kind of questions do they ask?" Brezhnev inquired.

"Well, for example, here's one I heard: 'I am a son of my father but not me. Who am I?' " the official proceeded to relate.

"I don't know," confessed Brezhnev.

"It's my brother," proudly announced Kosygin.

The next day, Brezhnev saw his foreign minister, Gromyko. "I have a riddle for you," said Brezhnev. "I am a son of my father but not me. Who am I?"

"I give up," the veteran Soviet diplomat muttered.

"Kosygin's brother, of course," exclaimed the Soviet leader.

*Question:* What are the four things wrong with Soviet agriculture?

*Answer:*    Winter, spring, summer, and fall.

A seven-year-old girl was staring at the stream of overseas visitors entering one of those well-stocked Moscow stores that accept only Western currency. A stranger approached.

"Pardon me, little girl," he asked, "what are you thinking about?"

"About what I want to be when I grow up," she replied.

"And what's that, may I ask?" the stranger inquired.

"A foreigner," the child replied.

As a result of the widespread criticism leveled at the USSR for its abuse of psychiatry, the Kremlin decided to permit a high-level delegation of Western psychiatrists to tour the most infamous of all Soviet institutions—Moscow's Serbsky Psychiatric Institute. It is here, the Westerners alleged, that mentally healthy political prisoners have been subjected to maltreatment.

To entertain the visitors, a large group of patients gathered in the Institute's courtyard. They sang Soviet songs hailing the arrival of Communism and the leading role of the Communist party. Noticing one silent person, the head of the visiting delegation approached.

"Why aren't you joining in the singing?" he inquired.

"I'm not certified crazy like the others. I just work here," came the reply.

An international polling agency decided to conduct a comparative opinion survey. They sought out an American, an Israeli, a Pole, and a Soviet.

"Excuse me, we're conducting a poll on the shortage of meat in your country," the pollster informed each of the four.

"What's a 'shortage'?" the American asked.

"What's 'excuse me'?" the Israeli asked.

"What's 'meat'?" the Pole asked.

"What's a 'poll'?" the Soviet asked.

A hare noticed a rabbit rushing panic-stricken into a forest outside Moscow.

Eventually catching up with him, the hare breathlessly asked, "What happened?"

"Haven't you heard? A new rule has just been announced. Rabbits with three or more testicles have to undergo an operation. No more than two testicles are permitted," the rabbit replied nervously.

"So if you're running like this, I assume you have more than two yourself," the hare concluded.

"No, but in this country, they cut first and count later," the rabbit said, as he raced off again.

*Question:* What is the definition of a Communist?[12]

*Answer:* Someone who has read the complete works of Marx, Engels, and Lenin.

*Question:* And what is the definition of an anti-Communist?

*Answer:* Someone who understands the works of Marx, Engels, and Lenin.

A conversation between two surgeons was overheard in the operating room of a Moscow hospital. They had to make a difficult decision.

"Shall we treat the patient with our country's advanced medical techniques or shall we let him live?"

---

[12]According to *The New York Times* (August 21, 1987), this is another favorite of President Reagan.

Anxious to avoid the caricature of the ugly American, Mr. Smith decided to study some basic words and expressions in several languages before departing from his native Philadelphia for his first vacation in Europe. But to his surprise—and disappointment—he found that almost everyone he met spoke English quite well.

While in Helsinki, a travel poster offering a weekend excursion to Leningrad caught his eye. "Ah," he thought to himself. "Something a little more off the beaten path. Just what I need."

Once in Leningrad, he set about seeing the sights: the magnificent Hermitage museum, bustling Nevsky Prospekt, the canals and bridges that remind visitors of Venice. One thing he didn't want to miss was a visit to the famous Finlandiya train station, the scene of Lenin's return, after years of exile in Western Europe, to a triumphal welcome by thousands of workers, soldiers, and sailors in 1905. Mr. Smith noticed two policemen on a street corner and approached them.

"Excuse me," the American said in his clearest English, "could you please tell me where I can find the train station associated with Lenin."

The two uniformed men looked at each other and shrugged their shoulders. "Now is my change to break out of English," Mr. Smith happily thought. *"Excusez-moi, où se trouve la gare?"*

Blank stares greeted this second attempt.

*"Scusate, dove stă la stazione?"*

No reaction.

*"Donde esta la estación?"*

Nothing.

*"Wo ist der bahnhof?"*

This fifth and last attempt was no more successful than the earlier ones. Exasperated, Mr. Smith walked away, having given it his all and having failed.

No sooner did he leave, though, than one of the policemen turned to the other and said, "Ivan, don't you think it might be useful for us to learn a second language?"

"Why, Petya? Look at that fellow who just came over to us. He spoke five languages, and it didn't help him, did it?"

There's E.S.T.—Eastern Standard Time; and then there's R.S.T.—Russian Standard Time.

"You are listening to Odessa Radio," intoned the announcer. "At the sound of the beep, it will be exactly 7 A.M. B-e-e-e-e-p! For those of you who didn't have enough time to check your watches and clocks, I repeat: At the sound of the beep, it will be exactly 7 A.M. B-e-e-e-e-p!"

*Question:* Since the Chernobyl nuclear accident, what sits on a plate and glows?

*Answer:*   Chicken Kiev.

A man with an opinion must have a reason for it.

"What do you think, Ivan? Does our country really possess the hydrogen bomb?" Petya asked his co-worker.

"Absolutely not, Petya," Ivan replied without hesitation.

"But how can you be so certain?" Petya wanted to know.

"Because if the country did, then how come we've never found it on the black market?"

Even an idiot knows the truth once in a while.

The village idiot ran down the main street shouting, "It's a dog's life! It's a dog's life!" A militiaman arrested him.

"Please leave him alone," shouted some passers-by. "He's the village idiot."

"I know that," responded the militiaman, "but this time he's talking too rationally."

As he lay close to death, Stalin asked to see a priest.

"Father, I want to go to heaven."

"In that case, you'll have to call in all your enemies and ask their forgiveness," the priest told the dictator.

"Fortunately, Father, I have no enemies," Stalin replied.

"But how can that be?" wondered the priest.

"I killed them all," replied Stalin.

It wasn't long after the attempted assassination of Pope John Paul II that the first reports of KGB instigation of the plot appeared in the Western media.

"Not true," responded the Kremlin press spokesman to a question about the allegation from a Western reporter. "Anyway, our man only fired after the Pope shot first."

An American tourist in Moscow wanted to water the drooping plant in his hotel room.

"Don't do that," shouted the chambermaid as she burst into the room. "It only causes the microphones to get rusty."

A long-time Moscow resident was recounting to an American tourist the horrors of Stalin's Great Terror during the 1930s.

"You wouldn't believe it," the Russian tearfully explained. "People simply disappeared from their homes and offices. Countless people were killed."

"But it's unbelievable that something like that could happen," the American exclaimed. "Didn't anyone call the police?"

After World War II, a Soviet soldier on patrol in occupied Germany shot to death a local resident fifteen minutes before the curfew.

"Ivan, why did you do that?" his astonished friend asked. "The fellow still had fifteen minutes to get home."

"I'd seen that guy before," said Ivan, "and knew where he lived. There's no way he could have made it back to his house in less than twenty minutes."

In yet another effort to eradicate religious practice, the KGB sent its agents to the nation's churches on a Sunday morning. At one house of worship an agent noticed an elderly woman kissing the feet of a life-size Christ on the cross.

"*Babushka,*[13] are you also prepared to kiss the feet of the beloved general secretary of our great Communist party?" he asked her.

"Of course I am," came the immediate reply, "but only if you first crucify him."

Brezhnev was rushed to the emergency room of the Moscow hospital reserved for *shishki.*[14]

"What's the problem?" the surgeon on call asked the leader's aide.

"He needs immediate surgery to broaden his chest. He just received another medal from the government, and there's no place left for him to wear it."

An American tourist invited what he thought was a prostitute up to his Moscow hotel room. Little did he know about the usual truth of such "chance" encounters in the USSR.

After they had spent the night together, he turned to her and asked, "My darling, tell me how much money I owe you."

"Forget the money," she replied. "Just influence President Reagan to end support for 'Star Wars.'"

A regular customer at a Moscow cafeteria ordered his favorite dish of Russian-style ravioli.

---

[13]Grandmother (Russian).

[14]Big shots (Russian).

"Hey, what's this?" he shouted after being presented with the dish. "Why are they round and not square?"

"That's because of *perestroyka*," the waiter replied.

"And why are they only half-cooked?" the customer wanted to know.

"That's because of *uskoreniye*," said the waiter.

"And they're uncovered," the customer complained.

"That's because of *glasnost*," the waiter explained.

"Which country has the tallest building in the world?" a journalist asked Reagan and Gorbachev at their first joint press conference.

"We do," proudly responded the American president. "The Sears Tower in Chicago is 1,454 feet tall. That's 110 stories. From the top, on a clear day, you can see a good fifty miles in any direction."

"Wrong, Mr. President. The tallest building in the world is in Moscow. It's the KGB headquarters on Derzhinsky Square," Gorbachev corrected Reagan.

Reagan, stunned by this unexpected news, hurriedly consulted with his advisors. Upon investigation, it was discovered that the KGB building was only a few stories high.

The president confronted the Soviet leader with the news.

"Mr. Gorbachev, how can you possibly claim that the KGB building is the tallest in the world when my advisors assure me it's no more than a few stories high?"

"Because from it's roof one can see clear across the country to Siberia," Gorbachev replied.

# PART III

## Eternal Jewish Humor

Tseitelman rushed to the rabbi to ask him what to do about an appendicitis attack. The rabbi prescribed a regular dose of cabbage. Miracle of miracles, within three days, Tseitelman returned to the rabbi to advise him that he had been cured. The rabbi, extremely satisfied, wrote in his notebook, "If a man comes to you with a case of appendicitis, cabbage helps."

The next week Shapiro came to the rabbi with a case of appendicitis. The rabbi checked his notebook and promptly prescribed a diet of cabbage. Within a day, Shapiro was dead.

The rabbi again pulled out his notebook. Where it was written, "If a man comes to you with a case of appendicitis, cabbage helps," he added, "in fifty percent of the cases."

Abram sought the help of his rabbi.

"Rabbi, I quarreled with my wife today. She started shouting at me, then I began shouting at her. I even cursed at her, then she started cursing at me. How should I go about seeking a reconciliation? I don't even know at this point who's in the right," Abram sighed.

"You're obviously in the right," the rabbi declared. "Now forget the whole thing and go and live in peace with her."

An hour later, Sarah, Abram's wife, came to the rabbi. "Rabbi, I quarreled with my husband today. He started shouting at me, and then I started shouting at him. Who's in the right?" she asked.

"Of course you're in the right. Now forget it and everything will be just fine," the rabbi told her as well.

At the rabbi's side during both meetings was one of his young disciples. "But Rabbi," said the young man in exasperation, "you always taught me to seek the truth. But there can only be one truth, an objective, absolute truth. How could you possibly tell each of the quarreling parties that he was in the right?"

"And you, too, are in the right, my son," affirmed the rabbi.

Abram went to the rabbi to seek help. Someone had been stealing Abram's chickens and he didn't know what to do about it. The rabbi went to Abram's farm and drew the picture of a triangle on the door of the chicken coop. The next day, Abram returned to the rabbi and told him that the drawing hadn't helped; more chickens had been stolen during the night.

So the rabbi returned to the farm, and this time he drew a pentagon with a circle inside it. This didn't help either.

The rabbi agreed to pay the farm a third visit. This time he drew a hexagon with a triangle inside it. The following day, Abram returned to the rabbi to advise him that nothing had changed.

The rabbi was once again about to set off for the chicken coop when Abram told him there weren't any chickens left.

"Oh, what a shame," sighed the rabbi. "And I had so many more interesting drawings in mind!"

A rabbi and a Russian Orthodox priest had a car accident. Fortunately, neither was hurt, and the damage was minor. The rabbi, seeing this as a good opportunity to celebrate ecumenism, took out a bottle of brandy from the glove compartment. He poured a drink for the priest but insisted that he himself wasn't thirsty.

A few minutes later, the police arrived at the scene. The rabbi politely suggested that the priest was at fault; the priest equally politely suggested that it was the rabbi's fault. The police gave each a breath-analyzer test, then promptly accused the Russian Orthodox priest of drunken driving!

Two Jews were traveling by train from Kiev to Odessa. Neither knew the other. The younger of the two was very well groomed and had lots of packages with him, including a bag overflowing with several kilos of sausage.

"Are you Shapiro?" the older Jew asked.

"Yes I am," exclaimed the surprised younger Jew, "but how did you know? I've never seen you before."

"It was really quite simple," began the older man. "Traveling on this route with so many sausages, you couldn't possibly be going as far as Odessa, because it's easy to find sausage there. So you must be going to one of the small towns en route. It has to be a town with a large Jewish population, since you look Jewish. That means it must be Zhmerinka.

"For a young person like yourself to go to Zhmerinka can only be for one of two reasons, either a marriage or a funeral. Since no one has recently died in Zhmerinka, it must be for a marriage.

"I know of only two forthcoming marriages. One girl is marrying a hunchback, which obviously you are not, and the other is marrying a fellow named Shapiro! And that's how I knew who you are!"

Dr. Khaimovich was summoned to an emergency house call. By the time he arrived, the patient was dead.

"Did he perspire before dying?" he asked the dead man's wife.

"Why yes, he did, doctor," she replied.

"Fine. That's already a good sign then," the doctor assured her.

Two friends met on the bus.

"Khaim, did you hear that Abram had to have a glandular operation," Motel asked.

"Ay, ay, ay. And he had so much wanted to be able to have children!" Khaim sighed.

Khaimovich was riding on the tram. It was so crowded that it was difficult to keep his balance.

"Excuse me, but you're holding on to my beard," said the man standing next to Khaimovich.

"Don't worry about it," replied Khaimovich. "I'll be getting off in a few stops."

Here's a pointed question and a pointed answer.

"Abram, is it necessary to ask so many questions?"

"And what else would you like me to ask?"

The Kogans waited for years to purchase a car. Finally, their turn came, but luck wasn't on their side. Within a few days they had an accident, which was duly reported to the police. The case was soon brought before the court.

"Who was driving your car?" asked the judge.

"I was," answered Sarah Kogan.

"Really? But all the witnesses testified that your husband was driving," the judge challenged.

"No, it's not true," Sarah protested. "He was only sitting behind the wheel, but I was driving," she asserted proudly.

Abramovich and Khaimovich were competitors in the coffin-making business in Berdichev. One day a man walked by Khaimovich's shop.

"Come in and have a look around," Khaimovich said. "Maybe you'd like to buy a coffin for a dearly beloved."

"No, thank you," somberly responded the man. "I've actually just ordered one from Abramovich."

"How could you?" Khaimovich asked in dismay. "His coffins are so small that your dearly beloved won't even have the chance to stretch her elbows once in a while."

Solomon and his son Abram lived in forced exile in a remote village in Siberia. Life was difficult enough for them, but when Abram died, Solomon, an impoverished and elderly man and the only Jew in the village, found it impossible to bear. So he decided to write God a letter and ask God to send fifty rubles per month to make conditions more tolerable for him.

The letter, however, fell into the hands of the postal authorities. They, in turn, handed it over to the local militia. The militia discussed it with the district officials, and it was agreed that if Solomon was really in such desperate straits as to write to God, then maybe it would be best to give him a monthly allocation. The sum of twenty-five rubles was agreed upon.

The next day a militiaman was sent to Solomon's house. "Sign here," ordered the militiaman.

"For what?" asked Solomon.

"I have a payment of twenty-five rubles for you," he replied.

Solomon sighed, took the money, and promptly sat down at his table to write a letter. That evening the postal authorities discovered another letter from Solomon to God. It read: "Dear God, Thank you very much for the money. But next time, please don't sent it via the militiaman. He stole half of it."

In Russia, everyone minds his own business.

"Khaimovich, your wife is sleeping with another man behind the pile of wood," his friend Yankel whispered.

"Whose pile of wood is it?" Khaimovich asked.

"Birnbaum's," was the reply.

"Then go speak to him about it," Khaimovich suggested.

Everything is relative, even in the USSR.

"Khaim, did you hear that Einstein is coming to visit Odessa?" Moishe asked.

"And who is this Einstein?" Khaim responded.

"He's a famous scientist, most noted for his theory of relativity," Moishe explained.

"What's that?" asked the ignorant Khaim.

"Let' see, how can I explain it to you?" Moishe pondered. "I'll give you an example. If you have three hairs on your head, is that a lot or a little?"

"A little," was Khaim's reply.

"And if you have three hairs in your bowl of soup," Moishe continued, pleased with himself for being able to clarify the matter, "is that a lot or a little?"

"A lot. And Einstein has to come all the way here to Odessa to explain this *'wisdom'* to us?" Khaim said in astonishment.

Poor Rabinovich, the shop manager! With every passing month, the authorities made him pay ever higher taxes. But to everyone's surprise, Rabinovich complied without a murmur. Months passed in this manner, until one day Rabinovich entered the tax office carrying a big box. He set it on the floor and started to walk out again.

"Excuse me, but you seem to have left this box here," said a tax officer. "Don't you need it?"

"No, I thought it best to leave it with you. It'll be much easier all the way around. This way instead of having to call me in every month and asking me to pay higher taxes, you can just use the equipment in the box to print the money yourselves," Rabinovich said as he hurried away.

Khaim found an empty seat in a restaurant and ordered a brandy. A few minutes later, he ordered the same for the couple at the next table, then for a couple at a third table, then for the headwaiter, and finally for the waiter. After a while, Khaim got up and started to leave.

"And who's going to pay for the brandy?" asked the waiter.

"Sorry, but I don't have any money on me right now," replied Khaim.

The waiter pounced on Khaim, beat him up, and threw him out on the street. The next day, Khaim returned to the restaurant and again ordered some brandy from the same waiter.

"And I suppose you want me to bring some brandy to the couple at the next table, right?" asked the waiter.

"Yes, please," Khaim said.

"And some brandy for the couple at the other table?" the waiter continued.

"Uh-huh," Khaim said.

"And some brandy for the headwaiter?" the waiter went on.

"Right," Khaim said.

"Okay. And some brandy for me?" the waiter asked.

"No," came the unexpected response.

"But why?" protested the waiter.

"Because you start fighting when you begin to drink," Khaim promptly replied.

Khaimovich ran out to the pharmacy at 3 A.M. and frantically began to knock at the door. After a while, the pharmacist came out in his pajamas and robe.

"What do you want at this hour?" asked the sleepy-eyed shop owner.

"Do you by any chance have any ink for sale?" inquired Khaimovich.

"No, we don't," said the annoyed pharmacist.

Khaimovich returned home, searched his apartment, and returned to the pharmacy a few minutes later.

"What do you want now?" shouted the pharmacist.

"Well, I just found a bottle of ink at home and came by to bring you some," responded Khaimovich.

Khaim, a nosey sort of fellow, was always asking personal questions of his friends.

"Abram, after all these years of marriage, do you and your wife still sleep in the same bedroom?" inquired the curious Khaim.

"Actually, we don't," Abram admitted. "We sleep in separate rooms."

"What happens if your wife wants to make love with you?" Khaim queried further.

"She whistles," Abram replied.

"And if you want to make love with her?" Khaim pushed his friend's patience to the limit.

"Then I shout out: 'Sarah, have you whistled yet?'" Abram replied.

What would a husband say if he returned home and found his wife in bed with another man?

If he were French, he'd say, "I'll kill both of you," pull out a gun, and shoot his wife and her lover.

If he were English, he'd say, "I'm so ashamed," go into the next room, and shoot himself.

If he were Russian, he'd say, "Mashka, you're here fooling around with Petka while they're selling eggs at the shop. Get your bag and hurry over there."

If he were Jewish, he'd say, "How could you possibly exchange me for a Russian?" To which his wife would gleefully reply, "But Khaim, I've just discovered he's also a Jew!"

In Russia, intermarriage was a problem too.

"Listen, Abram," said Khaim, "I think it's time for your sixteen-year-old daughter to get married. I've got the man for her."

"I hope he's a Jew," Abram replied.

"Well, actually, he isn't, but he would make a wonderful husband. He's a count and extremely rich. Sounds good, huh?" asked Khaim eagerly.

"I don't know," hesitated Abram. "I think my daughter ought to marry a Jew."

"What are you talking about? I tell you, he's perfect for her. Besides, he's part of the nobility and has lots of money," Khaim persisted.

"Mmmm, maybe you've got something there. Okay, it's a deal. When can the wedding take place?" the father asked.

"I'll let you know. All I have to do now is find a wealthy count who's prepared to marry your daughter," the *shadkhan*[1] said, as he scampered off to find the perfect man.

In the days of the last czar, Jews were not permitted to live in the major urban areas of Russia without permission. Khaim was able to obtain a permit, but his friend Abram could not. One day, they were standing on a city street corner when they noticed a policeman walking toward them.

"Abram, he's coming this way. What should we do?" asked Khaim, fearful for his friend.

"Mmmm, let me think. Aha, I know," said Abram. "You start running, and he'll run after you. Since you've got permission to be here, nothing can happen to you. That'll give me time to get away."

So Khaim began running. Predictably, the policeman set off after him. Several minutes passed before the policeman finally caught up with him.

---

[1]Matchmaker (Hebrew, Yiddish).

"Hey you," barked the policeman, "what's the idea of running like that? Wait a second. You're a Jew, aren't you? I can always tell Jews. I bet you don't even have permission to be here."

"But I do," protested Khaim, pulling out the official paper.

"So if you have permission, then why were you running?" the policeman demanded to know.

"My doctor suggested that I run as a way of strengthening my heart," Khaim said, thinking quickly.

"But didn't you see me running after you? Why did you think I was running?" asked the confused policeman.

"I assumed you had the same doctor," Khaim replied without hesitation.

Khaim and Abram met just prior to their emigration at the turn of the century.

"How's your English?" asked Khaim.

"I speak fluently," replied Abram in Russian.

"What can you say?" inquired Khaim enviously.

"*Bonjour, madam*," said Abram.

"But that's French," protested Khaim.

"My God, I didn't realize I also spoke French," exclaimed Abram.

A gift is a gift — sometimes.

"Abram, what did you bring me from Paris?" asked his wife Sarah.

"I don't know, dear. I haven't been to the doctor yet," the husband sheepishly answered.

Khaim was close to death. All his relatives gathered at his bedside.

"Khaim, do you have a last wish?" asked a relative.

"Yes. Call the Russian Orthodox priest," Khaim whispered weakly.

"But why?" the relative asked, surprised by Khaim's request.

"Because I want to convert to Orthodoxy," Khaim said.

"For what possible reason?" all the relatives demanded in a shocked tone of voice.

"So that when I die there will be one Russian less," muttered Khaim.

Shapiro was riding with a friend on the train and staring at a well-dressed man sitting opposite him. He was trying to figure out where the man might be going.

"He couldn't possibly be returning home for a concert or play because it's too late at night," Shapiro whispered to his friend. "That means he must be going to his mistress."

"But in this direction there are only two good-looking women available—Sarah and my wife. Since I myself am now headed for Sarah's place, he must be going to see my wife. My wife has two lovers—Khaimovich and Rabinovich. I know Khaimovich well, so he must be Rabinovich."

He approached the fellow sitting opposite.

"Hello there, Rabinovich!" Shapiro said cheerily.

"But how did you know my name?" a startled Rabinovich asked.

"The power of deductive thinking!" Shapiro smiled.

Shapiro worked as the assistant director of a factory, Ivanov as the director. Both were married men. In great need of a secretary, they hired a voluptuous-looking woman who knew very little about typing but certainly added luster to the office. It wasn't long before both Shapiro and Ivanov were seeing her separately, during lunch and after work, respectively.

Within a short time she was pregnant and nine months later she gave birth. On that fateful day, Ivanov had a meeting, so he couldn't go to the hospital immediately, but Shapiro went. When he returned, Ivanov was anxious for news about his secretary's health.

"How is she? Was it a boy or girl?" Ivanov asked.

"Actually, she had twins," said Shapiro. "Mine died shortly after birth, but yours is doing just fine."

Khaim and Abram met in New York one year after their emigration.

"Khaim, can you speak English now?" asked Abram.

"A *bissl*,"[2] replied Khaim.

Khaim volunteered for service in the Russo-Japanese War in 1905. One week later, Kogan arrived at the same camp to which Khaimovich had been assigned.

"Is the battlefield far from here?" asked Kogan.

"It's difficult to say," replied Khaimovich. "It takes me two hours to reach there in the morning, but I manage to make it back here in the evening in ten minutes."

---

[2]A little (Yiddish).

When Khaim and Sarah's son was six years old, they decided he should leave Berdichev to live with a highly cultured Russian family in Kiev. Khaim visited the family and was deeply impressed by the beautiful Russian they all spoke. Now, at least, his son would learn to speak proper Russian, not the Yiddish-tinged Russian, with its distinct intonation and accent, characteristic of such heavily Jewish towns as Berdichev.

Six months passed before Khaim decided to go to Kiev to see how his son was doing. At the house of the Russian, he was met by the tall, patrician head of the family who said to Khaim, "So vat d'ya vant?"

Abram sought the rabbi's counsel.

"Rabbi, my wife is betraying me. I don't know what to do," he wept.

"Perhaps you should think of divorcing her," advised the sage.

"But we have two children who wouldn't understand what was happening if we divorced," the husband countered.

"Then you should try to resolve the problems between you," advised the rabbi.

"But every time she sees a man, any man, she begins to flirt with him, even if I'm standing right next to her," Abram complained.

"Then perhaps you should divorce her, and try and explain it to the children in terms of incompatible personalities," the rabbi suggested.

"But where would I find another woman who cooks as well, who keeps such a clean house, and who is as good a mother to my children?" Abram wondered aloud.

"Then try to settle your differences, Abram," the rabbi urged.

"But can you imagine that since the day of our marriage she has had one lover after another," Abram observed.

"Then it would be best to seek a divorce," said the rabbi, his tone of voice beginning to rise in frustration.

"But . . ." Abram began to protest again.

"You know what, Abram. I've got the perfect solution. Why don't you convert to Russian Orthodoxy?" the rabbi said with finality.

"But how could that possibly help my situation?" Abram asked.

"It won't," admitted the rabbi, "but it will certainly help mine. You can drive the priest *meshugge* instead of me."

A girl came home from school.

"Mama, today in school we were told that each child should come to class tomorrow wearing his or her national costume," she said.

"Khaim, can you believe it?" asked the astonished mother. "At the age of 11, our daughter already needs a mink coat."

You'll know who's the boss in this story.

"Khaim, go and close the door," ordered his wife Sarah.

"Not now, Sarah. I'm reading," the husband replied.

"Khaim, you have four choices. Either you go and close the door, or I'll slap you in the face three times," she shrieked.

Circular reasoning can make your head spin.

"What are you thinking about, rabbi?" an elderly Jew asked.

"What am I thinking about? I'm thinking about why there is the letter 'I' in the word 'happiness.' " the rabbi replied.

"But, rabbi, there is no letter 'l' in the word 'happiness,' " protested the old man.

"Yes, but I'm thinking about what would happen if there was the letter 'l' in the word 'happiness,' " said the rabbi.

"But why, rabbi?" responded the old man.

"That's just what I'm thinking—why?" repeated the rabbi.

The great Jewish minds came together to consider the question: What is the most important part of the human body?

Spinoza argued that it was surely the mind. The power to reason was the essence of life itself.

Jesus insisted that it was the heart. Without the capacity to love, what would be the sense of living?

Marx claimed that the stomach was the most important part of the body. If a man were hungry, he was capable of anything.

Freud said that most important of all were the sex organs. They shaped the entire personality.

And Einstein declared that everything was relative.

Time puts everything into perspective.

"Abram, did you know that Napoleon died?" Yankel asked.

"Oy, but he was never sick," moaned Abram.

"He died about 150 years ago," Yankel said, annoyed that his friend was so ignorant.

"My God! How quickly time flies!" Abram muttered, shaking his head.

The facts of life in a Russian classroom.

"Abram, why weren't you in school yesterday?" asked the teacher.

"Because I had to take our cow to mate with a bull," the lad replied.

"But couldn't your father do it?" the teacher inquired.

"Yes, I suppose so," said the boy, "but he says that it comes out better with a bull."

Khaim was the only survivor of a shipwreck. He managed to reach an uninhabited island, where he spent several weeks without seeing any sign of life. One day, though, he saw another ship pass, then start to founder. He swam out, managing to rescue a beautiful woman. Back on the deserted island, the woman expressed her gratitude to Khaim.

"Oh my savior, I'll do anything for you, anything," she purred. "Just tell me what it is you want, and I'll give it to you in a way that only I know how. Tell me."

"Passover is coming. You didn't by any chance happen to bring some *matzah*, did you?" he asked eagerly.

*Tzures* all the way around.

"What shall I do?" one Jew asked another. "I'm really desperate. My son has converted to Christianity."

"I don't know, but I'm sure the rabbi will have some advice for you," assured his friend sympathetically.

Later, in the rabbi's office, the father pleaded, "Rabbi, help me. My son has converted to Christianity. What shall I do?"

"I'm sorry but I can't help you," the rabbi sadly responded. "You see, my son has also converted. Let's go and speak to God."

In the presence of God, the two distraught fathers tried to find solace. "God, you must help us," pleaded the two men. "Both of our sons have converted to Christianity."

"I'm afraid I can't be of much help to you," said God. "In fact, my son has also converted to Christianity."

Khaim was near death. All his relatives assembled at his side.

"Is my beloved wife here?" whispered Khaim.

"Yes, my dear," she said, tears streaming down her face.

"And is my lovely daughter here?" the dying man asked.

"Yes, papa," said the young woman, her voice choked with emotion.

"And is my son-in-law present?" Khaim asked weakly.

"Right here, Khaim," replied the son-in-law.

"Oh my God! Then who's looking after the shop?" asked Khaim.

Abram was from Odessa, Khaim from Moscow. The two met for the first time during Abram's visit to Moscow. They hit it off so well that Abram invited Khaim to visit his home.

"How will I find you when I get to Odessa?" asked Khaim.

"Simple. You go to Pushkin Street, number 155, enter the courtyard, and shout 'Abramovich, Shapiro, Kogan.' All the sixty windows except one will open. That'll be mine. I'm Rabinovich."

Abram was given the chance to visit Paris, but before leaving his hometown of Berdichev he went to his friend Khaim to seek advice.

"Khaim, what am I going to do? I don't speak a word of French," Abram said anxiously.

"Don't worry, Abram. All you have to do is speak Russian and put a 'la' before every word," Khaim reassured his friend.

Abram arrived at the train station in Paris and promptly shouted, "la taxi." A taxi came right up. He got in and said, "la restaurant," and the driver took him to a restaurant. He went in, sat down at a table, signaled the waiter, and ordered "la borscht." The waiter brought him the beet soup, which Abram happily wolfed down.

He again signaled the waiter and suddenly began to speak to him in Russian. "Isn't it amazing," said Abram, "that everyone in Paris understands me?"

To this the waiter replied in Russian, "If I wasn't 'la Jew' from 'la Berdichev,' then you would have just eaten a bowl of 'la *dreck*'[3] instead of 'la borscht.' "

Moishe ran up to Abram on the street, waving his arms to catch his friend's attention.

"Abram, did you hear the news? Khaim is dead," Moishe shouted.

"Alive, dead, what's the difference—so long as he's healthy," Abram replied, and without a second thought, he continued on his way.

---

[3]Garbage (Yiddish).

Two Jews, Moishe and Khaim, were sitting in the public baths.

"Khaim, I'm not well," Moishe sighed.

"And who's well, Moishe?" replied his friend philosophically.

"Khaim, I'm *really* not well," Moishe replied emphatically.

"And who's *really* well, Moishe?" Khaim countered.

Suddenly, Moishe gasped and dropped dead. Khaim was in a state of shock. Rushing to the lifeless body, Khaim grabbed him by the shoulders, shook him, and said, "But Moishe, why didn't you tell me you were feeling even worse than the rest of us?"

Izya walked into a pet shop in Moscow to buy a parrot. The shop manager pointed out a particularly unusual parrot.

"Do you speak English?" Izya asked the parrot.

"Yes," replied the parrot.

"And French?" Izya continued.

"*Oui*," the bird said.

"And German," Izya challenged.

"*Ja*," said the parrot, showing off.

"And Yiddish?" Izya asked.

"Of course! I grew up in Berdichev," said the parrot indignantly.

In Berdichev at the turn of the century, two friends met on the train.

"Khaim, what a nice suit! Where did you get it?" Moishe asked.

"In Paris," Khaim replied.

"Where's that?" Moishe inquired.

"It must be at least 2,000 miles from here," Khaim guessed.

"Can you imagine that? Such a nice suit from such a God-forsaken place," said Moishe in amazement.

Khaim went to Moscow from Kiev to collect the 6,000 rubles that he had in the bank there. Unable to return to Kiev until the next day, he spent the night in the apartment of his friend Abram. Before going to bed, Khaim told Abram that he'd like to put the money in a safe place for the night and that he'd like a third person present. Abram invited his neighbor to act as a witness. The next morning, Khaim asked Abram to retrieve the money.

"Money, what money?" asked Abram.

"Why, the 6,000 rubles that we put in the cupboard over there," Khaim replied nervously.

"I don't remember putting any money in the cupboard," Abram said.

"What? Where's the money?" demanded Khaim, beginning to feel queasy. "We had a witness. Let's call in your neighbor."

Abram went to get him. "Weren't you a witness to the fact that my 6,000 rubles were hidden in that cupboard over there last night?" Khaim asked the neighbor. "Tell us the truth."

"Uh, uh, I didn't see anything. I don't know what you're talking about," stammered the neighbor, who then hurried out of the room.

Abram took a key out of his pocket, opened the cupboard, removed the 6,000 rubles, and handed the money to Khaim.

"But Abram, why did you have to give me such a fright? I almost had a heart attack," Khaim sighed with relief.

"Well, Khaim, I just wanted to show you what kind of neighbor I have," Abram smiled.

A case of mistaken identity or hiding from oneself?

"Khaimovich, look at you. A new suit, new hairdo, fancy airs about you," said an elderly acquaintance.

"Excuse me, but I'm not Khaimovich," protested the man.

"Oh tut, tut. . . . And now you aren't even Khaimovich either," muttered the old-timer.

A group of men were discussing the age at which a woman reaches her prime.

"Eighteen," said one.

"Twenty-five," declared another.

"Thirty-one," announced a third.

"Thirty-seven," insisted a fourth.

"No, you're all wrong," said Abram. "It's my Sarah. She's seventy-eight. Every time she makes love with me she thinks it may be the last. You should only see what magnificent scenes she creates!"

Abram and Khaim met on an Odessa street. Khaim was carrying a watermelon.

"Khaim, can you tell me where Pushkin Street is?" Abram asked.

"Abram, hold this watermelon, please," requested Khaim.

Free of the watermelon, Khaim shrugged his shoulders, threw up his hands, and exclaimed, "And how should I know?"

Rabinovich, Abramovich, and Shapiro met to discuss who was the most important of the three.

"Listen," began Rabinovich, "I went on holiday to Yalta last summer, and I wasn't there more than a few hours before I was being paged to the telephone. Who was it? Gorbachev himself. He said: 'Rabinovich, get back to Moscow immediately. We're at a loss without you here in the Kremlin.'"

"That's nothing," said Abramovich. "Last month I had to go for business to the United States. No sooner did I arrive at my hotel in New York than there was a message waiting for me. It was from President Reagan. He asked me to come to the White House to advise him on world affairs."

"A mere trifle, my friends," said Shapiro. "When I was in Rome last year, I met with the pope. After our meeting, he invited me to join him at a press conference. The first question, from a well-known Italian journalist, was addressed to me: 'Excuse me, Mr. Shapiro, but would you be kind enough to introduce us to that funnily dressed guy standing next to you?'"

Sarah finally managed to get a job as a guide in an Odessa art museum. To make life easier, her standard explanation of the paintings was quite simple: "All the naked women are Venuses, and the ones with clothes on are Madonnas."

There are at least two ways of looking at everything.

"My husband has such willpower, you wouldn't believe," boasted Sarah. "Ten times already he's wanted to quit smoking, but somehow he manages to resist."

Bernstein met his friend Kogan.

"How are things?" asked Bernstein.

"Bad, I've got cancer," Kogan said sadly.

"That's not so serious. Don't worry about it," urged Bernstein.

"Really? Do you really think so?" Kogan said, anxious for any words of encouragement.

"Of course. Look, *I* have cancer. Now *that's* serious!" Bernstein explained.

Grinblat went to the doctor. He was desperately in need of a medicine to control hyperactive behavior.

"What could you possibly need such medication for?" asked the doctor. "As it is, you're emaciated and sickly."

"It's not for me," pointed out Grinblat, "it's for my wife."

Khaim was explaining to a friend why he always bought shoes two sizes too small for him: "You see, I come home from work after wearing those shoes all day long. I take them off, and I feel as if I'm in paradise."

Moishe worked as a train conductor on the route between Moscow and Odessa. On one run, a passenger who had to get off at an intermediate station at 4 A.M. asked Moishe to wake him up fifteen minutes before.

Unfortunately, Moishe did not. The passenger himself only woke up after the train was an hour past the stop. As he prepared to get off at the next town, he cursed Moishe's absentmindedness and stupidity. The other passengers felt sorry for the conductor and did their best to console him.

"It's just terrible the way that fellow attacked you," said one passenger.

"You think *he* was mad?" replied Moishe. "You should have seen the one I did wake up at 3:45 and sent off the train at the stop back there. Now that man *really* cursed at me!"

Khaimovich arrived late for the concert and clumsily made his way to his seat. As he sat down, he whispered to his neighbor, "What are they playing now?"

"Beethoven's Fifth," replied the neighbor.

"That's good," said Khaimovich. "Then I've only missed the first four!"

There's a reason for everything.

"Khaim, can you come over tomorrow night?" Abram asked.

"I'm sorry, Abram, but I can't. Shapiro is playing the violin," explained Khaim somewhat obscurely.

"How about the night after?" suggested Abram.

"No chance. Shapiro is again playing the violin," Khaim begged off.

"Tell me, what's he going to be playing at the performance?" Abram inquired, impressed by his friend's interest in music.

"I have no idea, but every time he plays, I sleep with his wife,"
Khaim smiled.

A rabbi and a bishop shared a train compartment. Just before going to
sleep, the rabbi asked the train conductor to wake him up a few
minutes before his scheduled midnight stop. As requested, the conductor woke up the rabbi at the desired time.

Not wanting to disturb his fellow cleric, the rabbi got dressed in
the dark, but by mistake he put on the bishop's garments. He then
went to the toilet, caught a glimpse of himself in the mirror, and
exclaimed, "*Oy vay iz mir.*[4] The conductor woke up the wrong person!"

A flying saucer landed in the Ukraine. An extraterrestrial being got
out to look around. Within a few minutes, he came across a local
resident.

"How are things around here?" the newcomer inquired.

"All right," gasped the man, "but who are you and where are you
from?"

"I'm a space traveler from another galaxy," the alien explained.

"What a beautiful coat of gold thread you have. Do all your
people have such coats?" inquired the man.

"Yes, and why not?" said the extraterrestrial being.

"And the pants are also made from gold thread, aren't they? Can
everyone afford such pants?" the man asked in amazement.

"Of course," came the reply.

---

[4]Loosely translated as "Oh, my goodness!" (Yiddish).

"But what is that stone you're wearing around your neck? Is it a diamond?" the astonished man persisted.

"Yes," the strange-looking being responded.

"And can all your people afford diamonds, too?" asked the man, fascinated by the visitor.

"No, only we Jews," was the reply.

Khaim and Abram were waiting at the train station.

"Listen, Abram, I'll bet you twenty rubles I know why you're going to Kharkov," Khaim said.

"You're on, Khaim. Why?" asked Abram, doubting that his friend could win the bet.

"To buy nails at five rubles a kilo and sell them back in Berdichev at twenty rubles a kilo. After all, there aren't any nails for sale in the whole town," Khaim explained, certain he was right.

Abram reached into his pocket, pulled out twenty rubles, and handed them over to Khaim.

"You see, I told you I knew why you were going to Kharkov," boasted Khaim.

"In fact you didn't, but the idea is certainly worth twenty rubles to me," said Abram as he boarded the train.

Two beggars were sitting in front of a Russian Orthodox Church. One looked Jewish, the other appeared Russian. All the worshippers entering the church gave a few kopecks to the second person; the Jew got nothing.

"I don't understand why you're sitting here," said a passer-by to the Jewish-looking beggar. "How can you expect to make any money? Why don't you go beg in front of the Jewish church if you know what's good for you?"

"Khaim," said one beggar to the other, "get a load of what this woman is saying. She thinks she can teach us!"

Khaim was in need of the best medical advice. He left his native Odessa for Moscow, where he was examined by a leading specialist. After the medical visit, he went to the telegraph office to send his wife a cable. He composed the following text: DOCTORS SAY OPERATE OPERATE, KHAIM, and brought it to the clerk. The clerk pointed out that he had repeated the word "operate" twice. That was precisely the way he wanted the telegram sent, Khaim explained.

The clerk, immediately suspicious, sought the advice of her supervisor. He couldn't make anything of it but suggested that the telegram be sent in the hope that a response could shed light on the affair.

In fact, a few hours later, a telegram for Khaim arrived from Odessa. It read: DOCTORS SAY OPERATE OPERATE, KHAYA. This was too much for the telegraph employees. And so they referred the whole matter to the police. Khaim was promptly summoned to police headquarters and asked to explain the mystery surrounding the telegrams. Was he sending coded messages? Was he in touch with foreign agents?

"No, no, it's none of that," he patiently explained. "It's actually all very simple. My telegraph should be read as follows: DOCTORS SAY OPERATE. OPERATE? KHAIM, and my wife's response: DOCTORS SAY OPERATE? OPERATE. KHAYA."

Poor Khaim! Together with his wife, twelve children, and in-laws, he lived in a tiny, cramped bungalow on a small plot of land in a Ukrainian village. Surrounded by a few goats, cows, and chickens, Khaim and his family eked out a marginal existence.

When Khaim's wife gave birth to the couple's thirteenth child, the problem of space became simply too much for Khaim. Consequently, he decided to consult the local rabbi.

"Rabbi, I just don't know what to do. I can't deal anymore with the lack of space in our house. Between my wife, the children, and my in-laws, there's hardly any room to get about," Khaim complained.

"I've got just the solution for you, Khaim. I want you to go home and bring your goats, cows, and chickens into the house," the rabbi told him.

"But rabbi. . . ." Khaim began to protest.

"Khaim, just do what I say," the rabbi said firmly.

Khaim followed the rabbi's advice, but soon found the new situation even more intolerable. He resolved to return to the rabbi.

"Rabbi, it's awful now, just terrible. Don't you have any other advice?" begged the distraught man.

"Yes, Khaim. I want you to go home and put the animals outside again," ordered the rabbi.

So Khaim did, and the next day he was back at the rabbi's. "So how are things now, Khaim?" the sage asked.

"Oh rabbi, I can't even begin to tell you. Since we moved the animals out, we've got so much space for our family. You're a genius!" shouted Khaim, clapping his hands in delight.

The rabbi was presented with another dilemma. "Rabbi, you're the only one who can help us to resolve our dispute. We're building a *mikve*.[5] Half the community says that we should polish the floor, and the other half says that we should leave the wooden floor as it is. Who's right?" demanded the chairman of the building committee.

---

[5]A ritual bath (Yiddish).

"Mmmmm, it's obvious you're both right. You should polish the wooden floor and then install it upside down," was the rabbi's reply.

A sign in the waiting room of Khaimovich's Odessa bordello: "Our customers always come first."

What was Khaim to do? Year after year his wife gave birth, and Khaim just didn't have the money to support such a large family. As was customary, he decided to seek the advice of the rabbi.

"Rabbi, help me. I just can't deal with still more children," Khaim confessed tearfully.

The rabbi consulted the Talmud before offering advice. "Khaim, the Talmud says that in such cases one testicle of the man should be removed," the rabbi observed.

And so Khaim had one testicle removed, but his wife continued to have more babies. He returned to the rabbi. "Rabbi, what should I do? My wife is still having children," he sighed.

The rabbi again consulted the Talmud. "Khaim, the Talmud says that in such cases the second testicle of the man should be removed," the rabbi counseled.

And so Khaim had his other testicle removed, but his wife continued to have more babies. Khaim again visited the rabbi. "Rabbi, my wife continues to have children. What shall I do?" he begged.

The rabbi studied the Talmud a third time. "Khaim, the Talmud says that in such cases the testicles of the wrong man have been removed," said the rabbi bluntly.

Sarah took her newborn son to be circumcised.

"Tell me, what do you do with that foreskin?" she asked the *mohel*.[6]

"It's used to make handbags," he told her.

"And how much do these handbags cost?" she inquired.

"One hundred rubles," he replied.

"One hundred rubles! Isn't that expensive for a handbag?" Sarah asked in astonishment.

"For a handbag maybe, but all you have to do is rub it a bit, and it becomes a suitcase," the *mohel* said.

A man was walking along the street looking for a watch repair shop when he saw a store window with some watches and clocks on display. He entered.

"Can you repair my watch?" he inquired of the man behind the counter.

"No, I'm afraid we don't deal with watches here. We perform circumcisions," the proprietor explained.

"Circumcisions? Then why do you display watches in the window?" asked the would-be customer.

"And what would you like us to display?" was the store clerk's reply.

Shapiro went to a doctor to complain about sexual difficulties.

"Sometimes, doctor, I'm unable to get an erection," he confessed.

---

[6]Ritual circumciser (Yiddish, Hebrew).

"Tell me in detail about your sexual life. Are you married?" the doctor asked.

"Yes," Shapiro replied.

"And how often do you make love with your wife," the doctor continued.

"Six or seven times a week," Shapiro replied.

"And do you have any mistresses?" the doctor asked.

"Twice a week I make love with a typist in our office," Shapiro admitted.

"And is that all?" the doctor probed further.

"No. Several times a week I sleep with my neighbor," Shapiro added.

"Well, now I can see why there are times you don't get an erection. It's obvious you're making love so often that it may be too much for you," the doctor concluded.

"Ah, so that's why. And I thought it might have been because I masturbate four or five times a week," Shapiro sighed with relief.

The prospective newlyweds, Abram and Sarah, were waiting in the lobby of the Marriage Palace for their families to arrive.

"Abram, it's cold in this room. Please go and close the window," she asked sweetly.

"Yes, my dear," he replied lovingly.

A few minutes passed. "Abram, now I'm suffocating from the heat. Please go and open the window," she smiled at him.

"Certainly, my beloved," he smiled at her.

A few minutes passed. "Abram, I'm freezing to death. Please go and close the window," she said, fluttering her eyelashes.

"Of course, my pearl," he said, bowing graciously as he got up once again.

A few minutes passed. "Abram, I'm sweating so. Please go and close the window," she asked.

"Sarah, my dream, why don't we pretend the ceremony is over and we're now husband and wife. Isn't that a nice thought?" Abram asked, weary from opening and closing the window.

"Oh yes, Abram, it is," Sarah said with delight.

"Good. In that case, you can go and open the damned window yourself," he said, refusing to budge from his seat.

In a Jewish school during czarist times.

"Who was Moses?" the teacher asked.

Silence.

"Doesn't anyone know who Moses was?" she asked, shocked at getting no response.

"He was the son of the Pharaoh," suggested Abie.

"What! Aren't you ashamed of yourself? Don't you know that the Pharaoh's daughter went to the river's edge and found a child there who was Moses?" she asked.

"Teacher, how naive of you. That's only what she says," Abie replied.

An elderly woman and a young man were sitting next to one another on an Odessa tram.

"Excuse me, young man, but are you Jewish?" she asked.

The young man ignored the question and continued reading his newspaper.

"I asked you if you were Jewish, young man," she repeated a bit louder, thinking he might not have heard her.

The fellow went on reading.

"Couldn't you please tell me if you are Jewish," persisted the elderly woman.

"Yes, yes," said the young man with obvious irritation. "If you must know, I am Jewish. Now please leave me alone and let me read my paper."

"But that's funny," said the elderly woman.

"What's funny?" the young man asked.

"You don't look Jewish!" the old woman exclaimed.

Khaim and his parrot boarded the bus. In a short-time, the conductor approached to ask Khaim whether he had already bought a ticket. Khaim ignored the question and looked out the window at the river they were crossing.

The conductor asked a second time but Khaim continued to ignore her. Finally, the conductor, rapidly losing her patience, said to him, "If you don't answer me, I'll throw your parrot into the river below."

The parrot quickly turned to Khaim and said, "Khaim, for God's sake, pay the ticket. You know I can't swim."

Khaim returned home from work one day. His wife Sarah greeted him at the door.

"Sarah, I've got a terrible problem," Khaim began. "Our factory director and my supervisor both have lovers. They told me that if I don't find a lover, and soon, I run the risk of losing my job. They figure the more employees who have lovers, the fewer the chances that anyone will squeal on anyone else. Sarah, what shall I do? You know how difficult it would be to find another job."

"Khaim, if you must, you must. Do anything you have to not to lose your job," Sarah consoled him.

Several weeks later, Khaim and Sarah were walking down the street. From the opposite direction, three women approached them.

"Sarah, look. You see the woman on the right. She's our director's mistress. The woman on the left is my supervisor's. And the woman in the middle is mine," Khaim pointed them out.

"Well, I must say, Khaim, that *ours* is the nicest," Sarah replied proudly.

Abram and Sarah went shopping at one of the outdoor markets in Moscow. They approached a man selling chickens.

"Sarah, the guy is asking five rubles for a chicken. That means he hopes to get four, but will sell it for three. Sarah, give me two rubles," Abram said.

"Hey," he shouted, turning to the man, "will you sell me a chicken for one ruble?"

During a pogrom, poor Khaim was nailed to the door of his shop. The next day, Ivan was passing by when he noticed the crucified Khaim.

"Are you in pain?" asked Ivan.

"Only when I laugh," replied Khaim.

After emigrating to the United States with his wife at the turn of the century, in the wake of pogroms in the Ukraine, Abramovich quickly found a job and began sending a portion of his salary to his relatives in

Berdichev. But a year later, after having his first child, he wrote to his relatives advising them that he could no longer afford to remit them money. A few weeks later he received a telegram from them: HOW DARE YOU USE OUR MONEY TO RAISE YOUR SON!

Abram and his wife had the rare opportunity to visit Paris at the turn of the century. Claiming he was anxious to visit some museums, he sent his wife off to do some shopping. But no sooner did they separate than he ran in the direction of the red light district.

"Could we spend a little time together," Abram timidly asked a pretty woman standing on a street corner.

"Of course, sir. That's why I'm here," she smiled at him.

"But the problem is I only have twenty francs to spend," he explained.

"Sorry, but for twenty francs, it's impossible to find something good here," she said and walked away.

And with that bit of disappointing news, Abram went to meet his wife. Later that evening, as they were strolling, they happened upon the same girl Abram had earlier approached.

"What did I tell you?" said the attractive Parisienne, looking at Abram's wife. "For twenty francs, it's impossible in Paris to find anything good."

*Question:* What is the difference between an Englishman and a Jew?

*Answer:*    The Englishman leaves and doesn't say good-bye; the Jew says good-bye and doesn't leave.

# PART IV

## Some True Stories

"Just think. If any of you has a child who is born in the United States, he or she can become the first Jewish president," explained the caseworker at an orientation session for arriving Soviet Jews in Vienna.

"But he would be the second Jewish president, not the first," protested a Kiev Jew.

"But who was the first?" the caseworker asked.

"Abraham Lincoln," was the reply.

"How do you know he was a Jew?" was the caseworker's response.

"Who else but a Jew would have the courage to name his son Abraham?" asked the emigré.

A Soviet Jew arrived in Vienna and asked for immigration processing to the United States to rejoin his brother in California.

"How long has your brother been in the States?" asked the social worker.

"About a year and a half," he said.

"And how's he doing?" the social worker continued.

"Fine. He's working as an engineer and earning 1,500 dollars a month," said the emigré proudly.

"And how's he adapting?" the questions continued.

"Just fine. He's earning 1,500 dollars a month," he repeated.

"But, I mean, how's he doing psychologically, spiritually. Does he feel at home?" The social worker tried to clarify the question.

"Listen, what are you talking about? The guy made 150 rubles a month as an engineer in Odessa, and now he's making 1,500 dollars a month. How badly off can he be?" the man shrugged his shoulders.

At a briefing for Soviet Jews in transit in Rome, the social worker was explaining that Soviet economists would have little chance of working in their speciality in the United States.

"But why?" asked an economist in the group.

"Probably because the Americans are afraid you'll make the same mess with their economy as you did with the Soviet economy," interjected another emigrant.

At Moscow's airport, during the obligatory customs inspection for all emigrants.

"You can't take that picture with you. I must confiscate it," the customs official insisted.

"But it's only a post card of the British Houses of Parliament," protested the emigrant.

"That's what you say, Jew-traitor. And how do I know that it's not really a picture of a secret factory in Siberia?" the official sneered.

A family of very recent arrivals from Odessa sought out their friends who had earlier emigrated and were now settled in Brooklyn.

"What advice can you give us?" asked the newcomers.

"Go to the local Orthodox synagogue, speak to them a few words in Yiddish, and tell them that it's always been your biggest dream to become an observant Jew. Tell them that you only want to eat kosher food," the Brooklynites advised.

"But why should I say that? You know it's not true," said the newcomers, shocked at the suggestion that they lie.

"Because they'll go right out and buy you a second set of dishes for your kitchen," was the immediate reply.

"Why do you want to resettle in Australia? Isn't it far?" an American asked the Kiev engineer.

"That's just the point. It's nice and far—from both Moscow and Washington," the engineer explained.

The Soviet Jew was so anxious to be accepted for resettlement in Canada that he spent several days before the consular interview trying to anticipate the possible questions and formulating responses to them. When the time for the interview came, he was first asked the predictable questions about name, age, education, and profession. The consul then steered the direction in an unexpected path.

"Tell me, please, why do you want to go to Canada rather than to Israel?" was the next question.

The emigrant was at a loss for a response. Finally, he blurted out, "Because I want to live in a country without any anti-Semitism and where my children can truly grow up as Jews."

"Citizen, you are not permitted to take that book by Pasternak with you," the Moscow customs official advised Mr. Fridman.

"And why not?" Fridman asked.

"Because it's proscribed in the Soviet Union," the official replied.

"But I'm not going to the Soviet Union. I'm going to Israel," Fridman protested.

"You're still not permitted to take it. After all, how do you know it's also not proscribed there?" the official cautioned.

"Do you consider yourself an immigrant or a refugee?" the doctor from Kiev was asked.

"Neither," he replied. "I think that we can't conveniently be placed in either of the two categories. A third category is necessary for us—refujews!"

Ostia Lido, a beach resort near Rome, has become the temporary home of many Soviet Jews in transit to North America, Australia, and New Zealand. In Ostia, the main post office fronts on a large square. During the evenings, Soviet Jews gather there to chat, exchange information, analyze the latest rumors, and create new ones. The square has become so identified with the Soviet migrants that Ostia residents have taken to calling it Piazza Rossa—Red Square!

"I'm unable to take the train to Rome tomorrow. I have kidney trouble," explained the elderly emigrant from Lvov, who had recently arrived in Vienna.

"In that case, you must go to the doctor and be examined before we can take you off the departure list," answered the social worker.

"And where is the doctor's office? In this building?" the ill man asked.

"No. In fact, it's in another part of town," the social worker responded, determined that the man comply with regulations.

"If that's so, then I think I'll leave for Rome tomorrow," he said.

"But why? Aren't you ill?" the bewildered social worker replied.

"It'll probably kill me to *shlep*[1] all the way across town not knowing the language or where I'm going. I think I'd just rather live with the kidney pain," he said, a tone of resignation in his voice.

Bus #1 goes from the Ostia Lido train station to Lungomare Duca degli Abruzzi, an area of Ostia heavily populated by Soviet Jews. The locals refer to the bus as the "Russ-bus."

Customs officials at Chop, the border crossing between the USSR and Czechoslovakia, are accustomed to checking the large amounts of luggage that Odessa Jews carry by train on their way to Vienna. The luggage is often filled with souvenir items for sale in Western Europe to augment the paltry 120 dollars per person that exiting Soviet Jews are permitted to take.

When one young man indicated he had only one suitcase, the officials immediately became suspicious. They held him for two days, checked his suitcase four times, and subjected him to a thorough body search. Finally, in complete exasperation, the chief customs inspector

---

[1]Drag one's feet (Yiddish).

said to the young fellow, "Listen, you have my word—whatever it is you're smuggling will not be confiscated. Just tell me where you've hidden it."

"But I haven't hidden anything anywhere. Anyway, why do you think I'm smuggling something?" he asked.

"Because we haven't ever seen an Odessa Jew leave with fewer than fifteen or twenty suitcases," the inspector replied.

A half-Russian, half-Jewish Soviet emigrant was accepted for assistance, with her Jewish husband, by a Jewish voluntary agency in Vienna. The family wanted to proceed to the United States.

"Have you received your daily maintenance money from the cashier?" the social worker asked the family.

"Yes, we have. And now I would like to know the address of the voluntary agency that deals with Russian Orthodox emigrants," said the woman.

"But why?" asked the social worker.

"Because since I'm both Jewish and Russian, I should be getting full financial assistance from each group," she said in all sincerity.

Whenever officials of one of the Jewish voluntary agencies operating in Vienna doubted the Jewishness of an emigrant, they would pose a few questions about lineage, history, and religion. But the "Jewish telegraph" was functioning day and night. One day an arrival was being put to the test.

"How did you get the name Fyodorov?" asked the official. "It's a typically Russian, not Jewish, surname."

The emigrant proceeded to explain in great detail how bribes, self-hatred, careerism, and a mixed marriage here and there among his ancestors had led to the present state of affairs.

Still suspicious, the official moved on to the next phase—to determine the emigrant's Jewish knowledge by asking him to identify a few objects. Just as the official was reaching for the desk drawer, the emigrant remarked, "Don't bother. In the left drawer are a *yarmulke*[2] and *tallis*.[3] In the right drawer is a prayer book."

"When we submitted our documents for emigration to the Kiev OVIR," explained an emigrant, "the inspector dealing with our application, a lawyer by training, demanded that I produce a document verifying my statement that my parents were dead. But they had been killed by the Nazis in 1941 at Babi Yar.

"In fact, more than 30,000 Jews were mowed down in two days. Consequently, when I asked how I could possibly produce such a document, he looked surprised and said in complete seriousness, 'Didn't the German soldiers give a death certificate to your parents' surviving relatives at the time?' "

"Why did you leave the Soviet Union?" the Moscow fashion designer was asked.

"Three words," she hesitantly responded.

---

[2]Skull cap (Yiddish).
[3]Prayer shawl (Yiddish).

"Persecution of Jews?"

"No," she replied, "suggestion of friends."

"What differences do you find between Odessa and Vienna?" the social worker asked the recently arrived butcher.

"In Odessa we had money, but there was nothing to buy in the shops. Here we have no money, and there are so many things to buy."

"Was Harry Truman a Jew?" asked the emigrant.

"No," replied the social worker. "What gave you the idea he was?"

"Such a great man and not a Jew?" the emigrant pondered.

A young Soviet Jew from Leningrad arrived in Rome and asked to be processed for Australia.

"Why do you want to go to Australia rather than, say, America?" a friend asked.

"Well, you see," he explained, "if I'm an American and travel abroad, I'm immediately loved or hated by the local people precisely because I'm an American. I'd prefer to say that I'm from Australia and run the risk of people confusing it with Austria rather than being loved or hated automatically."

The Moscow International Book Fair takes place every two years. In 1981, at the cramped American Jewish exhibit of hundreds of books on Judaica, a large crowd gathered. Needless to say, this manifestation of interest in Jewish culture did not escape the attention of the KGB.

To keep a closer eye on the visitors and prevent the smuggling of books out of the hall, a nonuniformed agent was sent in. Keen to mingle and remain unobserved, the agent picked up a book in Hebrew from the shelves. Suddenly the Jewish visitors began to whisper to one another and move away from the man.

"There's a KGB agent here," someone muttered to one of the American representatives, pointing to a man now standing alone.

"But how did you know?" the astonished American asked.

"Easy. His assignment was clearly to mingle. But his bosses forgot to brief him on one important thing: When picking up a book in Hebrew, it should be read from right to left, not left to right."

At the same book fair, the authorities later assigned several uniformed militiamen to the American Jewish exhibit area.

"What are they doing here?" protested an American to an official. "We did not request their presence."

"They are here for your protection," was the official's reply.

"Against whom or what?" the American demanded to know.

"Against anti-Jewish provocations," the official said.

"By whom?" challenged the American.

"Look, there is no anti-Semitism in our country. Therefore, you, as Jews, are perfectly safe in the streets. But here in this pavillion, there are many other foreigners attending the fair. How do we know that among them there aren't anti-Semites?" the official solemnly asked.

Those Soviet Jews who arrive in Vienna on their way to North America are often lodged in a hotel called "Zum Turken." To reflect the anything-but-luxurious comforts the hotel offers them, the migrants have renamed the hotel "Zum Tukhes."

"Is it possible for us to be resettled in Alaska?" asked the newly arrived family from the USSR. "We like the climate and hear there's a lot of work available."

"Unfortunately, it's not possible," explained the migration counselor. "There is no organized local Jewish community in the state."

"Why?" they asked.

"Probably because it's too close to the Soviet Union," interjected another new arrival.

Overheard on the street in New York outside an exhibit on Soviet Jewry: "How misleading!" exclaimed a woman to her friend. "It said there was a Soviet jewelry exhibit, but I didn't see a single piece of jewelry inside!"

After spending a few days in Vienna observing how Jewish emigrants from Moscow and Leningrad looked down on Jews from the Ukraine, the patrician way in which Latvian and Lithuanian Jews conducted themselves, the manner in which those with higher education set themselves apart from the others, the complete isolation of the

Georgian Jews, and the pity with which Jews from European Russia looked at the Bukhara Jews from Uzbekistan and Tadjikstan and the mountain Jews from the Caucasus, one migrant commented, "For people from the world's first classless society, we are surely the most class-conscious people on earth."

When the Odessa Jew was advised at the Rome transit point that she had been accepted for resettlement in New York, she began to cry.

"What's the matter?" asked the social worker. "We thought you wanted to go to New York."

"No, no, you can't force me to go there. I absolutely refuse to get on the plane," she screamed.

"But where is it you want to go?" the social worker asked.

"Brooklyn, USA!" she said emphatically.

"Do you know the biggest irony of the emigration of Jews from the Soviet Union?" a recent arrival asked an American journalist. "In Russia we were called Jews. In the West we're called Russians."

*Question:* Why are there no more Jewish jokes in the Soviet Union?

*Answer:* Because Rabinovich, Khaimovich, and Shapiro have all emigrated.